Institutionalizing
the Grass Roots
in Brazil

CHANDLER PUBLICATIONS IN
POLITICAL SCIENCE
VICTOR JONES, EDITOR

_____

Science Research Associates, Inc., 259 East Erie Street, Chicago, Illinois 60611
Distributors   A Subsidiary of IBM

S R A

INSTITUTIONALIZING

THE GRASS ROOTS

IN BRAZIL

*A Study in Comparative Local
Government*

FRANK P. SHERWOOD

UNIVERSITY OF SOUTHERN CALIFORNIA

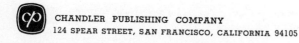

CHANDLER PUBLISHING COMPANY
124 SPEAR STREET, SAN FRANCISCO, CALIFORNIA 94105

TO

EMERY OLSON AND JOHN PFIFFNER,

GREAT INSTITUTION BUILDERS

CONTENTS

LIST OF TABLES AND ILLUSTRATIONS

PREFACE

Even in the case of a book as small as this one, it is quite a task to bring the results of many hours of research, writing, and rewriting to printed form. Inevitably, events and people affect the project from its origination to its final conclusion.

This book probably began in the fall of 1952 when I had the good fortune to serve as academic counselor to a group of eight Brazilians who were studying at the University of Southern California. Of this group, two had a special obligation to study municipal government and administration in the United States; and, as a result, we had a most rewarding relationship. Both went back to careers of distinction. One of them, Diogo Lordello de Mello, is quoted extensively in the following pages. He is clearly the outstanding authority on local government in Brazil. In addition to his scholarly activity, he has been most significant in doing the things necessary to institutionalize Brazil's municipalities.

In 1962 and 1963 I was privileged to have an assignment with a University of Southern California team in Brazil, under a technical-assistance program financed by the United States government. There, aided by Professor de Mello and many other friends, I renewed my earlier interest in Brazilian local government and began to collect materials. The pace in Brazil was hectic; there was much to be done and many fine people with whom to work.

It was back home at the University of Southern California that I first began to think about a book. But time on campus is not easy to come by. Fortunately, the enlightened sabbatical-leave policy of the University provided the necessary relief from other duties that enabled me to complete the first draft of the book.

Then another opportune event occurred. In 1965, the Inter-University Research Program in Institution Building (with the University of Pittsburgh, Syracuse University, Michigan State University, and Indiana University participating) made a grant to the University of Southern California to study institution building in Brazil. One of the two targets for these studies was the Brazilian Institute of Municipal Administration, of which Diogo Lordello de Mello was Executive Director. As a part of this research, in which Professor Aluizio Pinto has played the dominant role, it has been necessary to give particular attention to the municipalities and their development. If the municipalities do not prosper, there obviously can be little place for the Institute.

The pursuit of these studies gave me new ideas for this book. So back to the typewriter and the soft pencil.

But events are only part of the story. There must be a congenial environment in which academic people are encouraged and aided in their efforts to foster and transmit knowledge. For being able to do this at the University of Southern California, I want to express my gratitude to Henry Reining, Jr., Dean of the School of Public Administration. I also express appreciation to Alice Thibideoux, the hard-working, long-suffering secretary to the Dean, and my friend, for her support in a variety of essential facilitative tasks.

FRANK P. SHERWOOD

Los Angeles
February 1967

Institutionalizing
the Grass Roots
in Brazil

CHAPTER ONE

ABOUT THE BOOK AND BRAZIL

The problem of creating and retaining effective, representative, and dynamic political institutions at the local level is one which seems to transcend every governmental system.

Consider the matter for a moment. The population of the world is expanding at an awesome pace. Virtually all our social organizations are getting bigger and more complex. Indeed, bigness is becoming a way of life. Yet anything that is big is inherently cumbersome. Errors made at the top tend to proliferate and magnify as they proceed down through the system. Motivation is stultified by an individual feeling of helplessness and incapacity to affect organizational events. In short, depersonalization is typically a corollary to bigness.

In today's world the perils of bigness are compounded by the need for a high degree of technical specialization. The dinosaurs of the prehistoric past confronted a relatively simple and friendly environment; but the dinosaur passed from the scene as a more complex response became imperative. Similarly, there is a need to create social mechanisms that accommodate bigness and at the same time provide for highly specialized, individual contributions to the system.

Big cities are perhaps the best illustration of the problem. Large urban settlements existed also in earlier eras; but previous to a century ago there was nothing to rival New York City, Paris, London, and a few other metropolitan giants. Today we have cities that are bigger than ever before; and we have more of them. At the same time, life in the city has changed because of the technological revolution. Industrialization, communication, and transportation have all promoted a highly intensified pattern of role sharing in which no one individual does very much to provide the basic essentials to his own survival. We depend on each other.

1

Furthermore, the processes that foster interdependence show no signs of abating. In fact, the opposite is occurring. The affluent society requires increasing interdependence to meet such needs as traffic and pollution control. In the less affluent society, the push toward interdependence is seen in the demand for a community water system, collective disposal of waste, and the replacement of man and horse muscle by electric energy.

Thus bigness in the cities involves two things—more people and more things to do.

How do we create local institutions that avoid the fate of the dinosaur? Answers to this question are important not solely because the imperatives of modern urban life make the city the purveyor of essential services; they are perhaps even more significant because the cities represent a vital element in the political system, regardless of ideology. In the authoritarian, totalitarian organization, cities exercise their influence subtly. In the democratic society, they are the building blocks for the entire representative process. From the national perspective, vital local government can be an important deterrent to the stifling, stultifying effects of bigness.

Some societies appear to have been more successful than others in coping with these problems. Part of the reason may be found in political philosophy. The Anglo-Saxons built a considerable amount of localism into their concepts of government; or perhaps more accurately, their philosophy evolved out of the pragmatic requirements of British feudalism. Other societies, to the contrary, found their national identity through a process of authoritarian centralization.

In either case, however, the problem is roughly similar today. That is, all societies face the peril of bureaucratic atrophy through bigness; and in addition, the democratic societies are confronted by the task of rooting popular sovereignty in vital local institutions. However, different societies can use different prescriptions for the same problem. In the United States, for example, considerable popularity has attached to the notion that we have too much autonomy in our local institutions; and there is some tendency to favor assignment of tasks upward. Brazil, on the other hand, has fought the problem of how to develop participation, rather than limit it.

Though it may at first seem far afield from the interests of most Americans, the long-time Brazilian effort to create viable local governments contains an important lesson. It suggests how much local participation and concern should be prized and with what care we should approach fundamental changes in these traditions. It is interesting, and not a little frightening, that there seems to be a seductive appeal to integration and consolidation. While Americans have been loath to create large new levels of government, they have not been hesitant to delegate functions upward through financing and other arrangements. In Brazil lip service has been given to the strengthening of local governments, but actual behaviors have revealed substantial reservations. It is very difficult to build a faith in local institutions when they are impoverished, ineffective, and not very representative.

These opening paragraphs have sought to assign an importance to comparative studies of local government. The premise, in summary, is that all social organizations require vigor and a certain measure of independence throughout the system as a means of counteracting tendencies toward oligarchic bureaucratization. In the democratic society decentralization has particular pertinence as a contributor to the political process and as a safeguard against the loss of basic freedoms. The problem is to develop greater specificity with regard to these role imperatives, to understand the blocks that are really significant in opposing their fulfillment, and to develop viable institutional responses. To achieve these goals, the more comparative experiences we record and understand, the better.

Beyond contributing another country's experience, the case of Brazil deserves attention for other reasons. Not the least of these reasons is the importance of Brazil as a country. It is the Gargantua of South America, with more than one-third of that great continent's total population. Though it has experienced almost 150 years of independence, Brazil is still seeking its way governmentally; and it is certainly experiencing all the stresses of the developing societies. It is really no flight of the imagination to say that what happens in Brazil's urban environment can have a great deal to do with the fate of an entire continent.

Because it is so large and because of the idiosyncrasies of its economic and social growth, Brazil provides virtually every variant on the scale of municipal development and performance. It is certainly feeling all the pressures of rapid growth, with some of its biggest cities experiencing population increases as high as 10 per cent per year. In the south of the country this growth has been erected on a substantial industrial development; and the problems of these areas are becoming increasingly those of the affluent society—traffic, mass transit, public facilities, public utilities, and so forth. In the north, urban development is proceeding at almost as fast a pace. However, it is based far more on the push of the poverty-stricken rural areas than on the pull of industrial jobs. Similar phenomena have been observed in Africa and Asia, prompting the charge of overurbanization. What is interesting about Brazil is that both types of urbanization can be found in a single national context.

Brazil's size and diversity set it apart from many other countries in another respect: it is not a country with a single primate city, like Mexico, Argentina, Iran, and others. It possesses two of the largest metropolitan areas of the world, each with 5,000,000 people; and the 1960 census reported five other cities with populations exceeding 500,000. It has thus had to cope with metropolitan problems not only on a wide geographic front, but also in a variety of socioeconomic contexts as well.

It is curious, and somewhat paradoxical, that the complexities of the Brazilian socioeconomic setting do not appear in the governmental structure. In fact, another reason why the Brazilian experience proves to be especially interesting arises from the simplicity of the three-tier system of government, which embraces the national government, 22 states, and more than 4,000 municipalities. Aside from the territories, the Federal District of Brasília, and the state of Guanabara, these three levels function throughout Brazil. One major complication of this attempt to keep the structure simple is the delimitation of the municipality on a geographic, rather than an urban, service basis. As a result, the municipality is expected to meet rural as well as urban obligations, in direct contrast to the European and United States concept of the municipality as uniquely urban. Whenever such attempts at government simplification are made, we must expect stresses. The situation with regard to the municipalities in Brazil is no exception, as we shall see later.

Basic Data on Brazil

Before it is possible to consider Brazil's local government problems in depth, a minimum familiarity with Brazil as a national phenomenon is necessary.

First, a few notes about the significance of Brazil in the world and in the South American demographic setting. By 1966 Brazil had reached an estimated population of 85,000,000 people. Furthermore, it appears that most predictions of Brazil's population increase have been extremely conservative. There is a tendency to use the figure of 2.5 per cent per year, which was the average for Latin America and for Brazil during the 1950's. Actually, however, it is estimated that the growth rate in Brazil has been at the level of 3.6 per cent since 1958. Official predictions are at the rate of 3.4 per cent per year. On this basis, by 1970 Brazil's population will be about 95,000,000, which may be as much as 38 per cent of the total Latin American population.

Urbanization has been occurring at an accelerating pace in Brazil, though Brazilian census definitions tend to skew the population distribution toward an urban classification.[1] United States definitions, in contrast, are more stringent. Even so, it cannot be denied that the move toward urban living in Brazil is of major proportions. The 1950–1960 period showed a rate of urban growth of 63 per cent, in contrast to a 39 per cent rate during 1940–1950. The rate of rural growth, on the other hand, remained constant over a 20-year period at 16 per cent. Table 1 summarizes these data.

As a result, Brazil is quickly moving toward the time when the majority of its people will be city dwellers. In 1950 only about one-third of the Brazilians were regarded as living in an urban setting. A decade later the reported number had risen to nearly one-half, 45 per cent. And in 1965, the Brazilian population was about half urban, half rural. By the time of the 1970 census, when the total population is expected to be 95 millions, Brazil will likely have experienced, in a decade, a 72 per cent increase in urban population, and the nation will be 60 per cent urban.

It may also be noted that Brazil is following a demographic trend which is fairly general in Latin America, that is, big population increases occur largely in the urban areas. It is predicted that by the year 2000 Latin America will have a population twice that of North America, and larger than that of Europe, or the USSR, or Africa.

---

[1] Brazilian census definitions tend to have a bias toward the urban classification because the seat of every one of the more than 4,000 municipalities, some with less than 1,000 inhabitants, is categorized as urban.

TABLE 1. COMPARATIVE RATES OF URBAN GROWTH
IN BRAZIL AND IN THE UNITED STATES, 1940–1960

Year	Total population (millions)		Urban population (millions)		% urban population		% urban population increase	
	Brazil	U.S.	Brazil	U.S.	Brazil	U.S.	Brazil	U.S.
1940	41	131	13	74	32	57	—	—
1950	52	151	19	96[a]	37	64	39	21[b]
1960	71	179	32	125	45	70	63	30

Source: Data for Table 1 have come from several Brazilian sources, primarily from *Anuário Estatístico do Brasil 1964* (Rio de Janeiro: Instituto Brasileiro de Geografia e Estatística, 1964). The U.S. source is *Statistical Abstract of the United States 1963* (Washington: U.S. Government Printing Office, 1963).

[a] U.S. census definitions were changed in 1950, accounting for a larger number of people in the urban classification. Under the old definition, 90 millions would have been categorized urban and the percentage would have been 60 per cent.

[b] The U.S. rate of increase indicated is derived from a comparison of figures obtained under the 1940 definition, thus eliminating the distortion caused by a changed definition.

Economically, Brazil has made considerable progress. In the period 1948–1961 it was one of six Latin American countries whose economic growth rate exceeded 5 per cent; it actually averaged 5.8 per cent. Industrial production increased about 10 per cent per annum over the same period. Since 1961, however, Brazil has encountered problems.[3] In 1963 the growth rate was only 1.6 per cent, resulting in a per-capita decline in gross national product of nearly 2 per cent. However, for the period 1960–1964, growth was still at the rate of 4.3 per cent, indicating the nation's inherent economic strength.

The extent of industrialization in Brazil is further indicated by the fact that, as early as 1950, it ranked third among the 20 Latin American nations in the percentage of its urban population employed in industry. The percentages cited for that period were: Argentina, 8.1%; Uruguay, 6.7%; Brazil, 6.5%; and Chile, 5.5%.[4] On the other hand, more recent

[3] "The Brazilian record . . . shows a much higher rate of growth in the fifties than in the years after 1961. An intensive inflationary process appears to have created unusual financial problems and the growth in manufacturing which had largely taken the form of import substitution fell sharply. The last several years have seen a vigorous effort to reduce the inflationary spiral. The evidence would seem to suggest that, aided by stronger coffee prices, the economy began to move forward in 1965." *Development Assistance Efforts and Policies: 1966 Review* (Paris: Organization for Economic Cooperation and Development, 1966), pp. 22–23.

[4] "Changes in Employment Structure in Latin America, 1945–55," *Eco-*

data do not indicate that Brazil's magnificent industrial progress has provided jobs equal to the rising level of urbanization. Whereas urban population was increasing 54 per cent in the decade of the 1950's, the number of "operários" (blue-collar workers in industry) was rising only 22 per cent, from 1,177,000 to 1,509,000. As is being discovered in the United States, modern technologies have obliterated any relationship between levels of production and jobs created in industry.

The other complication has been the continued regional disparity in the distribution of Brazil's economic wealth. As of 1960, the northeast and its 20 million people had a per-capita income of $140, about half of the national average. The south, particularly São Paulo, far exceeded these averages. One Brazilian writer has suggested that the north and the northeast remain in a "traditional" economic stage; the center-east, with around 25 per cent of the population, is ready for "takeoff"; and the south, with about 35 per cent of the population, is in full development.[5]

Thus it seems fairly clear that the north and northeast are the economic problem areas of Brazil. However, Robock has argued that, economically speaking, the problem is not as great as many Brazilian policy makers seem to think. In the first place, he says, such regional disparities are common in all countries. Moreover, between 1955 and 1960 the Brazilian northeast had the fastest growth rate of any region in Brazil, increasing its income level per capita from 42 per cent to 50 per cent of the national average.[6]

Brazil's Sociopolitical Development

Perhaps the most significant aspects of Brazil's evolution as a major nation state are (1) its colonization by the Portuguese; (2) the absence of a pronounced frontier movement; (3) the resolution of

---

nomic Bulletin for Latin America, Vol. II, No. 1 (Santiago, Chile, February 1957), p. 40, as quoted in W. Stanley Rycroft and Myrtle M. Clemmer, *A Study of Urbanization in Latin America,* rev. ed. (New York: The United Presbyterian Church in the USA, 1963), p. 59.

[5] Helio Jaguaribe, *Tempo Brasileiro* (Rio de Janeiro: publisher not named, 1962), cited in Vamireh Chacon, "Pernambuco," in Themistocles Cavalcanti and Reisky Dubnic, *Comportamento Eleitoral no Brasil* (Rio de Janeiro: Fundação Getulio Vargas, 1964), p. 220.

[6] Stefan H. Robock, *Brazil's Developing Northeast* (Washington, D.C.: The Brookings Institution, 1963), pp. 6ff.

virtually all internal conflict with comparatively little bloodshed; and (4) the lack of any major external threats.

Brazil's settlement by the Portuguese, beginning in the early part of the sixteenth century, has undoubtedly had a profound effect on its development. The sea-faring Portuguese came from a notably small country, with a population of less than a million. Their interest was not so much in settlement and in a new way of life as in the generation of wealth for the homeland. It was an exploitative posture; and it was undoubtedly enhanced by the natural riches of the young country. The land produced luxuriant crops of sugar, cocoa, and later coffee, which were harvested by slaves from Africa. Later, in the eighteenth century, gold was mined in immense quantities and fortunes were made. However, the system was essentially a transient one. Governors came, enriched themselves, and left. In this situation there was little opportunity for the religious zeal, the insistence on creating the new society, and the resistance to Europe that was to be found in many of the colonial undertakings of the United States. It is also to be observed that Portuguese Catholicism imparted an ethic substantially different from the Protestant ethic characterizing settlements in much of the United States. Work was hardly seen as a means to salvation.

Undoubtedly Brazil's geographic character has had much to do with the absence of any real frontier movement. There is a long range of mountains that hugs much of the coast of the country; and the great Amazon basin is an uninviting swamp. Geologically, too, Brazil is an old country; and the lands in the interior have not been excessively fertile. On the other hand, when there were diamonds and gold to be had, no one seemed to have much trouble moving inward. In any event, Brazil has generally lacked whatever democratizing influence came from the frontier movement in the United States.

This pattern of development may have had very considerable significance for Brazil's local government institutions. We can observe strong centralizing tendencies in the Crown and in the Church; and we do not find any counterbalancing factors in the kind of independent isolation that characterized frontier life in the United States.

Differences between the United States and Brazil are further accentuated when factors of conflict and threat are considered. Danger is a major motivation for collective action. Brazil has had very few worries about its real estate; and therefore national survival has not been dependent in any great degree upon the capacity to function as an organizational unit. With regard to the frontier, too, there has been relatively little threat and hence little need for community action. The Indians have been docile and few in number. The climate is warm and enervating. In such a setting, survival could remain largely an individual or family matter.

Because of some of these elements in the environment, and undoubtedly others as well, Brazil has been a nation in which strong personal emotions find expression, but with relatively little bloodshed. It is a curious paradox and yet understandable. The forces in the Brazilian's life space have made him very much an individual; organized bloodletting involves sacrifice of much of this individualism and requires commitment to a collective ideal, neither of which is appealing to him. Thus Brazil enjoys a most enviable heritage. Without battle, independence was won, the slaves were freed, a king was overthrown, an old-guard elite was destroyed, a tough-minded dictator was ousted, the shattering resignation of a President was survived, and a weak and vacillating successor was sent packing to Uruguay. Not all good things, however, have salutary consequences. Compromise has become a virtual way of life in Brazil. Goals are not infrequently distorted to accommodate power realities. In short, the nature of public life is such in Brazil that wholehearted commitment to an ideal and willingness to sacrifice in pursuit of a social need are neither expected nor understood.

FEDERALISM

Brazil operates as a federal system; but its roots, as we have indicated, are essentially centralist.

In the colonial period the center lay in Portugal. The possibility of political action at the colonywide level was avoided in good part by the requirement that the provincial governors report directly to the Crown in Lisbon. In 1808, when the Portuguese king fled from Napoleon to the New World, Rio de Janeiro became the center of the empire. The pattern of centralization persisted, down through the days of the independent monarchy from 1822 to 1889.

With the promulgation of the Republican Constitution in 1891, the concept of federation assumed legal significance. The provinces now became states; and the devolution of some power from the center began. This pattern was abruptly ended in 1930 with the revolution led

TABLE 2. EXPENDITURES, RECEIPTS, AND DEBT
IN THE BRAZILIAN GOVERNMENT, 1962

Level of government	Expenditures 1962 (%)	Receipts 1962 (%)	Total debt 1962 (%)
Federal	53.5	46.5	71
State	39	45	29
Local	7.5	8.5	0[a]

Source: Raw data were obtained from Anuário Estatístico do Brasil 1964 (Rio de Janeiro: Instituto Brasileiro de Geografia e Estatistica, 1964), pp. 363, 373. Percentage computations by author.

[a] The last year in which the Anuário Estatístico reported a debt for the municipalities was 1961, when it amounted to slightly more than 5 per cent of the total. A large floating debt, which is a device for financing by inflation, has been a part of the central-government fiscal operations for a number of years.

by Getulio Vargas. Except for the 1934–1937 period, the Vargas dictatorship functioned as a centralized system until its overthrow in 1945. The Constitution of 1946, which was slowly abandoned after the revolution of 1964 and finally replaced in 1967, probably represented a high-water point of federalism in Brazil.[7] While observing the formalities of the 1946 Constitution, the post-1964 central government, through a variety of interventions and other pressures, substantially reduced the antonomy that the states and municipalities had enjoyed for the approximately two decades following the overthrow of Getulio Vargas.

By United States standards, however, the balance of power in Brazil has always hung heavily on the side of the central government. The 1946 Constitution assigned a wide range of functions to the national government; in addition, the nature of government financing has consistently given the central government a heavy hand. The extreme inflation of recent years only served to aggravate the situation. By printing money, the national government met its financial needs, but

[7] For a provocative treatment of federalism in Brazil (and the argument that Brazil is basically a unitary state), see Carlos Medeiros Silva, "Evolução de Regime Federativo," in Themistocles Cavalcanti et al., Cinco Estudos (Rio de Janeiro: Fundação Getulio Vargas, 1955), pp. 71–92. Silva, Minister of Justice in the government of Humberto Castelo Branco, was a principal architect of the new Brazilian Constitution adopted in January 1967.

TABLE 3. EXPENDITURES, RECEIPTS, AND DEBT
IN THE UNITED STATES GOVERNMENT, 1962

Level of government	Expenditures 1962 (%)		Receipts 1962 (%)	Total debt 1962 (%)
	Domestic	Total		
Federal	27	58	63	79
State	24	14	18	6
Local	49	28	19	15

Source: Frederick C. Mosher and Orville F. Poland, *The Costs of American Governments* (New York: Dodd, Mead and Co., 1964), pp. 44, 45, 64, 100.

it left the lower levels in a chronic state of poverty and dependence on the center. Not only did revenues generally fall behind expenditures, but the local governments were left with virtually no sources from which to borrow for long-term improvements.

Table 2, which gives receipts, expenditures, and debt for the three levels of government in 1962, probably tells more about the actual state of federalism in Brazil than many paragraphs of explanation.

These financial percentages may be compared with the same 1962 period in the United States (see Table 3).

The similarities and differences in the two tables are noteworthy. The dominance of the central government in the United States in securing resources, both through taxation and borrowing, is clearly evident. The role of the central government of Brazil does not appear to be quite so pivotal, partly because the use of inflation to finance governments is not revealed by the tables. Because of large defense outlays, United States federal expenditures far exceed those of the other levels; in Brazil, on the other hand, defense expenditures run only 13 to 16 per cent of the outgo of the national government.

Perhaps the major difference involves the apparent reversal of importance of the state and local governments in the two societies. In making such a judgment, the assumption must be made that money is power. If one level of government collects and spends more money than another level of government, a fairly strong case can be made that the latter level occupies the dominant position in the total system. From this perspective, the states in Brazil are seen to be far more pivotal than the local governments, in contrast to a more ambiguous situation in the United States. Table 3 reveals that the states and the local levels in the

United States collect about the same amount of money; however, through various types of financial assistance from the states and the federal government, the local levels have been assigned many service responsibilities that cause them to spend about twice as much. The scale of this local government activity is particularly observable when defense expenditures are eliminated. In these circumstances, the local units account for nearly 50 per cent of all domestic outlays by United States public agencies.

The Brazilian situation is quite different. It is apparent, for example, that the local governments in Brazil perform few services for the higher levels. Indeed, in 1962, the local governments collected a higher percentage of public revenues than their expenditures represented. Here again we see an effect of inflation, for it was the central government that ran up the major deficit through its printing-press operations. In great part because of such deficit financing for current operations by the central government, the situation of the local governments in Brazil deteriorated considerably between 1950 and 1962. In the twelve-year period, the local-level percentage declined from 12 per cent of the total public expenditure to 7.5 per cent.

To summarize, federalism is an important factor in the Brazilian government system; but the nature of the system, as revealed by financial indices, differs somewhat from the United States. In the United States, the central government gains much of its power because of its tax-collecting capabilities; in Brazil, the central government gains significance because of its direct-expenditure activities, which have been financed in part by inflationary means. The other major difference is to be seen in the financial importance of the states in Brazil, which leaves the local level in a vastly weakened position in contrast with the United States. In this respect, however, it is important to recognize that there were in 1962 about 92,000 units of local government in the United States (municipalities, counties, and various special districts), as contrasted with only the 4,000 municipalities at the local level in Brazil.

SEPARATION OF POWERS

The other basic organizing principle in the Brazilian government structure provides for a separation of powers among the legislative, executive, and judicial functions. Again, the model is much the same as that in the United States; and hence it may be said that both countries operate under the Presidential system.

The Brazilian experience with Presidentialism is more limited than that of the United States. To the extent that there was popular sovereignty under the monarchy, the prevailing pattern was more akin to that of the British Cabinet system. Since the 1891 Constitution, however, separation of powers has been an underlying principle of Brazilian government. As might be expected, the Vargas dictatorship was an exception. Dictators do not—and cannot—recognize the independence of the legislative body.

Also, from September 1961 to January 1963, a so-called Parliamentary system was instituted to accommodate the conflicts arising from the resignation of Jânio Quadros as President in August 1961. However, the President remained the dominant figure; and the experience was so frustrating that the citizenry voted to return to full Presidentialism in January 1963. Since the revolution of April 1964, the Presidency has been further strengthened; and, with the recess of Congress in October 1966, the power of the executive branch approximated the level achieved during the days of Getulio Vargas.

While the power of the executive branch has been somewhat strengthened since 1964, the fact is that the Brazilian Presidency has characteristically been the most significant of the three arms of government. The Supreme Court, on the other hand, has played a relatively minor part in making the great policies of the land, in contrast to the situation in the United States.

Most noteworthy is the fact that the separation-of-powers doctrine has been rigorously applied at all levels of Brazilian government. The 1946 federal Constitution required that the states organize themselves on this basis. In addition, the municipalities have legislative and executive branches that are elected independently and function separately from each other. Perhaps even more strikingly than at the federal level, it would seem that the state governors and the mayors of the municipalities occupy the center of the political stage within their own jurisdictions. This centralization may be partly due to a cultural heritage which personalizes the leadership function. In an earlier, rural day, it was the patron who watched over his flock, much like the plantation owner in the United States South. In the present urban times the political leader is expected to perform many of these same functions. Further, these cultural predispositions nourish a system of patronage rewards in the securing of political-party strength and power. The Chief Executive finds himself the central figure because he makes the personnel appointments, awards the contracts, and grants most of the favors. The rewards bestowed by the legislative body are relatively few; and even some of these depend on the goodwill of the Executive.

Perhaps surprisingly, this dominance by the Executive does not always add up to dictatorship. It may mean arbitrariness in certain areas. It has in many cases meant corruption. But since winning tickets generally involve a variety of negotiations, compromises, and commitments, few Chief Executives find themselves really free agents.

OTHER PRINCIPLES OF THE SYSTEM

The management of elections is essentially a national responsibility in Brazil. There is no distinction, for example, between voting eligibility for the three levels. If one is eligible to vote for President of the Republic, he is also free to take part in the election of the municipality in which he is registered.

Thus far, voting eligibility has been restricted by the national Congress to those who can pass a literacy test. As a result only about 22 per cent of the total population was permitted to vote in the 1960 election for President. Perhaps not surprisingly, the illiterates' right to vote has become a hot political issue in recent years. When one is eligible to vote, he is required to do so. However, in the 1960 Presidential election only about 81 per cent of those eligible went to the polls. Data reported later in the book indicate that the percentage of persons actually voting in some states is as low as 14 per cent of the total population. The percentage is highest in the industrialized states.

Candidates for office must be nominated by a political party and must carry this designation on the ballot. It is not possible to run as an independent. However, until 1964 Brazil boasted so many splinter parties—and they were eligible to present candidates anywhere in the nation—that party nomination presented no real block to the eager candidate. After the elections of 1965, however, the government abolished the traditional parties and created a two-party system. In the contests for Congress in the fall of 1966, the government party, the National Renovative Alliance, won the majority of seats.

While the government's action in eliminating the multiparty system has clearly aroused varied opinions as to its ultimate effect on the country's political development, it is interesting that it did tend to eliminate the troublesome tendency of electing minority candidates to office. This tendency had been present because of Brazil's commitment to a single-election system: The candidate with the highest number of votes, though it may not be a majority, is the winner. As an illustration, in the 1962 race for the governorship of São Paulo, Adhemar de Barros won 37.8 per cent of the votes and Jânio Quadros 24.1 per cent. A third candidate received 21.8 per cent. Though only a little more than one third of São Paulo's voters had supported him, de Barros thus became governor. It is not infrequent that this single-election system results in the election of a clear minority candidate. In the 1960 election for governor of Guanabara, the two leftist candidates polled 55.7 per cent of the votes while the winner, Carlos Lacerda of the conservatives, got 35.7 per cent. The same types of events have tended to occur at the municipal level.

Elections for legislative offices follow the principle of proportional representation. Candidates for the federal Congress, for example, run on a statewide ticket; and the number of seats allocated to any single party depends on the total number of votes polled by that party. Candidates are selected according to the number of ballots they have earned for their party. The same pattern holds true for state and municipal legislative bodies. Thus the concept of a single-district representation, so characteristic of United States and English politics, does not exist in the Brazilian system. As a result, the reference groups for individual political figures tend to be more diversified. Instead of being a spokesman for the west side of town, a councilman may be known as the friend of education, or of the Church, or of sports.

Elections in Brazil have traditionally been an exciting affair. Banners of every type are strung from all available standards. Walls and sides of buildings are defaced by scrawled names of candidates. The propaganda is ceaseless, and the cost of campaigning is mounting rapidly. The suspense of the campaign often continues for many days after election day; for the tallying must be done in public before many witnesses. Because the work goes on only during the day, close elections sometimes require two weeks before the winner is declared.

Summary

There are many unanswered questions about the role of local government in modern society—democratic or otherwise. In every complex society there is the need to decentralize; and this need implies some form of local autonomy. In the democratic society, the question of role is particularly crucial. Vital local institutions are in many respects the foundation stone of the pluralistic, free society. In explaining why much of their comparative research of political participation in five countries was focused on local involvement, Almond and Verba have stated:

. . . we examined our respondents' relations with their local community. We were interested in the extent to which respondents considered themselves to have some sort of responsibility to be active in their community—either in a formal or informal way; either in relation to local government or in relation to fellow citizens. The local community seemed to be a good place to begin, since political and governmental problems tend to be more understandable, the organs of government less distant, the chances of effective participation for the individual citizen greater on the local level than on the level of national government. It has, in fact, often been argued that effective democracy rests on the ability of the individual to participate locally, for it is only here he can develop some sense of mastery over political affairs. As Bryce put it (and as defenders of local autonomy have constantly argued), "An essential ingredient of a satisfactory democracy is that a considerable proportion should have experience of active participation in the work of small self-governing groups, whether in connection with local government, trade unions, cooperatives or other forms of activity.[8]

---

[8] Gabriel A. Almond and Sidney Verba, *The Civic Culture: Political Attitudes and Democracy in Five Nations* (Princeton: Princeton University Press, 1963), p. 164.

CHAPTER TWO

URBAN GROWTH AND ITS CONSEQUENCES

The concept of the city is generally considered to be synonymous with that of the municipality; and both words imply an urban life. Things are a little more complicated in Brazil, however. Because of the three-tier form of government, the municipality (the local-government tier) serves both urban and rural inhabitants. The concentration of political power in the urban communities and their far greater need for services tend to dominate decisions in the cities. Thus, while we must bear in mind that Brazil's local governments have the schizophrenic task of serving both urban and rural masters, it is the city where things get decided and where the tensions of modern life have brought grief to many governments. Hence our concern in this book with the city (though not a legal entity in Brazil) and this chapter's focus on aspects of Brazilian urbanization and its correlates.

Rapidly accelerating urbanization is one of the significant phenomena of our times; and it seems to have no regional, cultural, or economic boundaries. Quite rightly, those who are concerned with political behavior in the emerging societies have called attention to the importance of urbanization as a foremost conditioner of such behaviors. Beyond indicating its broad significance, however, there is relatively little specification of the ways in which this influence is felt.

There is a predisposition to associate urbanization with industrialization. The 1954 finding of Davis and Golden that there was a positive correlation coefficient of .86 between the two has often been quoted as evidence of this linkage.[1] More recently, Kuznets has ad-

---

[1] In their inventory of findings on human behavior, Berelson and Steiner quote approvingly from Davis and Golden in the following terms: "The degree of urbanization increases sharply as industrialization increases. It follows that those parts of the world still mainly in the peasant agrarian stage of economic

vanced data to show that there is a substantial, positive correlation between urbanization, industrialization, and per-capita income.[2] Our easy acceptance of association between industrialization and urbanization is also probably abetted by the experience of the Western industrial world, where factory and city seem inextricably tied.

However, as Davis and Golden took pains to emphasize in 1954, a case-by-case study reveals situations in which the "push" of the impoverished rural areas has frequently become a more significant cause of urban growth than the "pull" of job opportunities in the cities. Egypt has been regarded as "overurbanized" for this reason. Its city populations have grown without the economic base that the Davis-Golden correlations suggested was necessary.[3] Thus, there is considerable evidence that the urbanization process can take place independently of any substantial, concurrent growth in the economic base, which is most typically expressed in industrialization. Hoselitz has noted, "Although there is a high correlation between industrialization and urbanization, the development of towns and cities is not dependent upon the previous establishment of industries . . ."[4]

Kuznets suggests that industrialization does not have to depend on urbanization. Emphasis on the independence of the two processes, he says, is "useful." "Cottage industry," for example, may be far more appropriate in many societies; and such a level of technology does not require an urban setting. Furthermore, a highly technological society like the United States permits exurban, rural living for the more affluent of its metropolitan inhabitants.

---

development manifest the least of urbanization . . . as of 1950 the (Pearsonian) correlation between the degree of industrialization and degree of urbanization, as measured by our indices, was .86 . . ." Original source is Kingsley Davis and Hilda Golden, "Urbanization and the Development of Pre-Industrial Areas," *Economic Development and Cultural Change,* 3:6–26 (October 1954); quoted in Bernard Berelson and Gary A. Steiner, *Human Behavior* (New York: Harcourt, Brace, & World, 1964), p. 604.

[2] Simon Kuznets, "Consumption, Industrialization, and Urbanization" in Bert F. Hoselitz and Wilbert E. Moore, *Industrialization and Society* (n. p.: UNESCO-Mouton, 1963), p. 102.

[3] Davis and Golden, pp. 11ff.

[4] Bert F. Hoselitz, *Sociological Aspects of Economic Growth* (Glencoe: The Free Press, 1960), p. 161. Heberle has also noted that "much of the industrial development has been a consequence rather than a cause of city growth" in the South of the United States. Rudolph Heberle, "Social Consequences of the Industrialization of Southern Cities," *Social Forces,* 27:29 (October 1948).

Brazil provides a unique opportunity to probe these questions preliminarily. Besides the fact that Brazil is important because it is big, Brazil's size also permits it to encompass various stages and types of urban and industrial development within one national context; and such comparisons within a country seem to pose fewer methodological problems than those between Egypt and India, for example. Furthermore, such differences as do exist pose important policy-making dilemmas for Brazil as a whole. How they are handled can have considerable influence on the future of Latin America's largest nation.

Relationships between Industrialization and Urbanization

To identify the extent to which urbanization and industrialization have been associated in Brazil, we may construct two indices: one for industrialization and the other for urbanization. The Industrialization Index is obtained by establishing a percentage relationship between the total number of people employed in industry, both transformative and extractive, and the total population of the state. A complication in computing the Urbanization Index is the absence of official, published data on the exact numbers of urban dwellers in the states. However, information is available on the number of people living in towns over 10,000; and certainly residents of these communities can be considered urban dwellers. Though it differs from official census definitions in Brazil, such a criterion is frequently used in other societies to establish the dividing line between urban and rural life. With these data, the Urbanization Index can be established by determining the percentage relationship between the number of people living in towns with more than 10,000 population and the total population of the state.

An analysis of urbanization-industrialization relationships is reflected in Table 4.

It is apparent from Table 4 that there is generally a rough relationship between urbanization and industrialization, as we might expect. The coefficient of correlation is +.75, as contrasted with the +.86 arrived at in the previously cited Davis and Golden worldwide study. In the eight-state sample, the Industrialization Index and also the Urbanization Index are lowest in the state of Ceará. In contrast, São Paulo, with the highest level of industrialization, is second highest in urbanization. Only Guanabara, which is the city-state of Rio de Janeiro

TABLE 4. URBANIZATION-INDUSTRIALIZATION RELATIONSHIPS
IN EIGHT BRAZILIAN STATES

State	% increase in urban population 1950–60	% increase (or decrease) in number of industrial workers 1950–60	% urban industrial to rural industrial workers 1960	Urbanization Index[a]	Industrialization Index
Bahia (pop. 5,990,000)	52	20	80	19	8
Ceará (pop. 3,337,000)	51	−(37)	90	16	6
Guanabara (pop. 3,307,000)	36	6	99.6	97	54
Paraíba (pop. 2,018,000)	44	−(40)	85	21	8
Pernambuco (pop. 4,136,000)	47	−(18)	75	30	18
Rio de Janeiro (pop. 3,402,000)	65	35	79	25	32
Santa Catarina (pop. 12,974,000)	66	40	72	19	19
São Paulo (pop. 12,974,000)	53	50	80	48	64

Source: All data are from the official census reports included in the *Anuário Estatístico do Brasil 1963* (Rio de Janeiro: Instituto Brasileiro de Geografia e Estatística, 1963).

[a] The Urbanization Index is a percentage relationship of the number of people living in cities with more than 10,000 population to the total state population. The Industrialization Index is based on the percentage relationship between the number of people employed in industry (both transformative and extractive) and the total population of the state, but should not be regarded as an actual percentage.

and which has no rural hinterland of consequence, boasts a higher Urbanization Index than São Paulo. Aside from these poles, however, it is evident that a close relationship between urbanization and industrialization does not hold in all cases. The southern state of Santa Catarina, for example, has an urbanization level about the same as that of the state of Bahia; their degrees of industrialization, however, are vastly different. The state of Rio de Janeiro has a lower level of urbanization than the northeastern state of Pernambuco; yet its level of industrialization is almost twice as great.

The four northeastern states of Bahia, Ceará, Paraíba, and Pernambuco, show an average Industrialization Index of 10, whereas the four southern states have an Index average of 42. On the Urbanization

Index, the northeastern states are not so far outdistanced, with an average of 21.5 compared to 31 for three southern states. (Guanabara is excluded because of its unique urban situation.) The general conclusion that industrialization and urbanization are not necessarily twins is further supported by reference to the percentage of industrial workers to total population in the various states. Even though the northeastern states have a fairly high level of urbanization, they rank far below the states of Rio de Janeiro, Santa Catarina, and São Paulo in the percentage of industrial workers to total population. With the same Urbanization Index as Santa Catarina, for example, Bahia has only about one-third of the percentage of industrial workers. The state of Guanabara again is seen to be atypical.

Furthermore, the situation does not seem to be improving in the north; Table 4 indicates that the increase in industrial-worker population is almost completely restricted to the southern states.

Finally, it should be noted that by far the greatest proportion of Brazilian industry is to be found in the urban setting. Aside from Guanabara, the most rural state (Ceará) and the most urban state (São Paulo) report only 10 per cent of their industrial workers located outside urban areas. The situation is roughly similar in the other states, with the percentage of urban industrial workers varying between 72 and 85 per cent of the total.

These data seem to agree with the observations of others. Bazzanella, for example, concludes that the Brazilian experience does not support the thesis that urbanization is a consequence of industrialization. He suggests that a "reverse cultural lag" is operating, in which the values of the peasant have become increasingly modern and urban while technologies have failed to keep up.[5] Robock seems to arrive at much the same conclusion in noting that rural poverty and the scarcity of rural employment opportunities are major factors in the push away from the land to the city. The northeastern cities, with all their inadequacies, still possess more promise than the impoverished countryside.[6]

---

[5] Waldemiro Bazzanella, "Industrialização e Urbanização no Brasil," *América Latina,* 6:3–27 (January–March 1963).

[6] Stefan H. Robock, "The Rural Push for Urbanization in Latin America: The Case of Northeast Brazil," prepared for a symposium on "Urbanization in Latin America—The Rural Setting," May 21–22, 1964, mimeographed, 17 pages.

Industrialization, Urbanization, and Voter Participation

Brazil's mandatory voting law theoretically requires each eligible voter to appear at the polls. On the other hand, the size of the electorate is severely limited by restrictions on eligibility, particularly by the literacy test; only about 22 per cent of the total population held the franchise for the 1960 presidential election.[7]

This situation contrasts rather sharply with the experience in the United States. Correcting for the large number of people under 21 in Brazil, we find that the United States voluntary system elicited a proportionately larger number of voters in the 1960 Presidential election than that in Brazil in the same year. About half of those over 20 voted in Brazil, whereas 64 per cent of the adults in the United States cast a ballot in that year. In the 1962 legislative elections in Brazil and in the United States, however, the effect of the mandatory election requirement can be seen. The percentage of adults casting ballots in the United States dropped to 46, while the percentage of Brazilians rose to a level slightly higher than that in 1960.

In both countries there are marked differences in voter participation in the various states, despite the requirement of mandatory voting in Brazil. In the state of Mississippi in the United States, for example, only 26 per cent of the adults voted in the 1960 election, as contrasted with 71 per cent in California and 68 per cent in New York. The neighboring state of Alabama also had a similarly low level of voter participation. In Brazil, as Table 5 indicates, the variations were nearly as great, ranging from 14.4 per cent in the northeastern state of Pernambuco to 37.7 per cent in the central state of Rio de Janeiro. In general, the 1962 election statistics, covering national, state, and local contests, revealed that states in the north and northeast of Brazil had a small percentage of persons eligible to vote and that they used the franchise less. In 1962 the four southern states, on the average, had

---

[7] The 1960 election was the last for President in Brazil; João Goulart was elected Vice-President and succeeded to the Presidency in 1961; Castelo Branco was installed as a result of the April 1964 revolution; and Costa e Silva was elected in October 1966 by the Congress.

TABLE 5. VOTER PARTICIPATION IN RELATION TO URBANIZATION
AND INDUSTRIALIZATION IN EIGHT BRAZILIAN STATES, 1962

State	% of population eligible to vote in 1962	% of total population voting in 1962	% of eligible electors voting in 1962	Industrialization Index	Urbanization Index
Bahia (5,990,000)	20	14.8	74	8	19
Ceará (3,337,000)	26	18.7	74	6	16
Guanabara (3,307,000)	36	30.7	85	54	97
Paraíba (2,018,000)	19.8	15.3	76	8	21
Pernambuco (4,136,000)	20	14.4	71	18	30
Rio de Janeiro (3,402,000)	32.7	24	80	32	25
Santa Catarina (2,146,000)	30	25.8	86	19	19
São Paulo (12,974,000)	30	25.5	86	64	48

Correlation between voting eligibility and Industrialization Index, r = .74
Correlation between voting eligibility and Urbanization Index, r = .42
Correlation between voting performance and Industrialization Index, r = .64
Correlation between voting performance and Urbanization Index, r = .36
Source: Raw data are from *Anuário Estatístico do Brasil 1963*. Computations by the author.

almost twice as large a percentage of the population eligible as in the north, 30 per cent as compared to 17; and only 16 per cent abstained, as contrasted with 26 per cent in the north.

Many factors outside the scope of this paper have obviously caused this situation. Nevertheless, it is important to recognize the discrepancies that exist in the various parts of Brazil. The data in Table 5 reveal a fairly high positive correlation between the level of industrialization and both the eligibility to vote and interest in voting. This correlation is to be expected. Industries need literate people; and such persons are much more apt to be aware of the communications which heighten interest in election campaigns.

It may also be noted that the same degree of correlation does not exist between level of urbanization and voter eligibility or involvement. The direction of the correlation remains positive but is very much lower. This finding also seems reasonable. Urban areas house more literate people and communications are better; however, the data do provide evidence that the urban area with industrialization is not the same as the one without industrialization.

TABLE 6. RATE OF POPULATION INCREASE
IN MAJOR BRAZILIAN CITIES, 1950–1960

City	1950 population	% of state population	1960 population	% of state population	popula-tion in-crease	annual increase
Belo Horizonte	352,000	4.6	641,000	7.0	96	9.6
Belém	255,000	22.7	402,000	26.0	58	5.8
Curitiba	181,000	8.5	361,000	8.5	100	10.0
Pôrto Alegre	394,000	9.5	641,000	11.8	60	6.0
Recife	525,000	15.4	798,000	19.27	52	5.4
Rio de Janeiro	2,377,000	—a	3,307,000	—a	36	3.6
Salvador	417,000	8.6	655,000	11.0	57	5.7
São Paulo	2,198,000	24.0	3,825,000	29.4	73	7.3

Source: Raw data are from *Anuário Estatístico do Brasil 1963.* Computations by the author.

a The city of Rio de Janeiro is the state of Guanabara, which contains only .02 per cent of the land area of Brazil but has the highest population density in the country. As a result, much of the population growth in the greater Rio area has occurred outside the boundaries of the state of Guanabara; the population of the metropolitan area is estimated at more than 5,000,000 people.

The Influence of the Big Cities

A demographic factor with great social and political significance is the explosive increase in population in the big cities, the large metropolitan areas. In the short space of ten years, for example, the number of northeastern cities with populations over 100,000 grew from three in 1950 to eleven in 1960. As Table 6 indicates, the growth rate in the big cities has generally exceeded the average 54 per cent urban-population increase for 1950–1960. Excluding the city of Rio de Janeiro, whose territorial restrictions have caused much of its metropolitan growth to occur outside its jurisdiction, the populations of the seven big cities of Brazil have increased at a rate 30 per cent faster than the average national urban increase. The growth rates of certain of the big cities of the South—Curitiba (Paraná), 100 per cent; Belo Horizonte (Minas Gerais), 96 per cent; and São Paulo, 73 per cent— emphasize the importance of the pull of economic opportunity. These areas, where industrialization is pronounced, are experiencing the highest degree of internal migration.

Another datum of significance is the clearly expanding predominance of these great cities in relation to the rest of the state. In 1950, the seven cities (excluding Rio de Janeiro) in Table 6 had an average of 13.3 per cent of the total population of their states; in 1960 that average had increased to 16.1 per cent. Only in Paraná did the relationship between metropolis and hinterland remain stable; and it remained so because Paraná has been experiencing a tremendous economic boom in its western regions. Otherwise, it is notable that the big cities generally have been increasing their predominance throughout the nation, as much in the north as in the south. Judging by the annual rates of increase, this commanding position will be further enhanced in the future.

The two metropolitan giants of Brazil—Rio de Janeiro and São Paulo—have significance for this analysis. Once the government-headquarters city, Rio is now experiencing a rather rapid industrial growth and is second only to São Paulo economically. A very large percentage of the federal income tax is collected from these two centers. The two cities have about 10 per cent of the national population total, which is not a large percentage. In terms of political power, however, the situation is quite different. Much of this prowess obviously comes from the cities' economic position; but the literacy and social involvement of these metropolitan populations are also significant. The voting strength of Rio and São Paulo, for example, appears to be almost twice as great as one would anticipate from their population. In the 1960 Presidential election these two centers accounted for about 17 per cent of the national vote, even though their population percentage was only 10. Johnson has reported that data for the 1955 Presidential election showed that the city of São Paulo, with approximately 5 per cent of the total national population, cast about 8 per cent of the total vote.[8] The same type of relationship can be found at the regional level between capital cities and their hinterlands: Recife, with about 20 per cent of the state's population, cast approximately 30 per cent of Pernambuco's ballots in the 1962 election; Salvador, with 11 per cent of the population, accounted for 18 per cent of Bahia's ballots; and Fortaleza, with about 10 per cent of Ceará's population, had a voting strength of 15 per cent.

---

[8] John J. Johnson, *Political Change in Latin America: The Emergence of the Middle Sectors* (Sanford, California: Stanford University Press, 1958), p. 175.

The Political Consequences of Industrialization and Urbanization

The effect of Brazil's urban and industrial growth on its political behavior can now be considered. However, it must be emphasized that hard data are sporadic and difficult to find; and the curtailment of political activity since 1964 has undoubtedly had its effect.

The most prominent theme in the usual appraisal is that the urban population represents a fairly homogeneous agglomerate with a reasonably high degree of political consensus. The direction of this consensus, of course, has varied in considerable degree with the theoretical propositions of the analyst. It has been common, for example, to assign much of the political muscle of Getulio Vargas to his appeal to the urban working masses. Leeds has even suggested that all mass movements in Brazil have been "urban-directed" and "urban-industrial" in their orientation.[9] Johnson's theory of the "middle sector" as an increasingly important political force in Latin America also rests heavily on the urban phenomenon. He identifies six characteristics that have given the middle sectors some cohesiveness and continuity. One characteristic is their "overwhelming" urban aspect. He says, "Whether they are salaried persons, self-employed professionals or property owners and *rentiers;* whether they belong to the middle sectors because of their learning or their wealth, the members of the intermediate group are almost solidly urban." [10] Johnson declares further that the middle sectors are committed to policies "that promote urban growth and economic development and assign a disproportionately large per capita share of public revenues to the urban centers."[11]

To some extent, such propositions with regard to urban homogeneity have validity. People in the urban setting are undoubtedly more articulate in pressing for their demands. Furthermore, since our data make it clear that most industrial activity occurs in the cities, it should come as no surprise that urbanites put a high priority on economic

---

[9] Anthony Leeds, "The Brazilian Variant," in Joseph Maier and Richard W. Weatherhead, ed., *Politics of Change in Latin America* (New York: Frederick A. Praeger, 1964), p. 194.

[10] Johnson, p. 5.

[11] Ibid.

development and industrialization. Finally, it seems obvious that mass movements are urban-directed. Urban communities are administrative centers, the linkage points in communications networks—imperative for any kind of organization. It hardly is expected that a mass movement will be run from a farmhouse.

One must recognize that urbanization is not a totally independent event. The disparities in regional development in Brazil necessarily leave their mark on the tensions and pressures of urban growth; and this effect is most to be seen in the presence or absence of industrial development. With industry, there are jobs, and money to pay for the services urban dwellers are increasingly demanding; without it, many of the rural miseries are simply transferred to the urban setting. And, as we have seen, these kinds of variables greatly influence present-day voting eligibility and involvement.

The politically significant big cities have exhibited a pronouncedly greater predisposition to place themselves to the left of the political spectrum than have the suburbs and rural areas. A study of electoral behavior in Brazil during the 1962 elections provides particularly useful information on this point.[12] The volume contains data which permit useful analyses of the elections in five states, three in the north and two in the south (São Paulo and Guanabara). In four out of the five cases, the "leftist" candidate led the voting in the city. In the other instance, Virgilio Távora, regarded as the conservative, won the Ceará governorship by a more than two-to-one margin. However, only 4 percentage points separated him from the Labor Party candidate in the city of Fortaleza. Miguel Arrais of the Labor Party won the governorship of Pernambuco by 2 percentage points, largely by piling up a 63 per cent majority in the city of Recife. In Bahia the conservative candidate was the Labor Party nominee; he won the election by 6 percentage points but lost by 17 percentage points in Salvador. In the bitter São Paulo gubernatorial fight, Jânio Quadros, who was regarded as the most leftist of the three candidates, led the field in the city of São Paulo by a narrow margin, but lost the election. Similarly in the city-state of Guanabara, in the race for lieutenant-governor, the leftist-identified candidate garnered an 8-percentage-point margin over his more conservative opponent.

---

[12] Themistocles Cavalcanti and Reisky Dubnic, *Comportamento Eleitoral no Brasil* (Rio de Janeiro: Fundação Getulio Vargas, 1964).

Chacon, in commenting on the Pernambuco election, declared, ". . . the cities had a role still more important in the election than in 1958 . . . It can even be said that the victory of Arrais was, above all, urban . . ." [13]

Observers have pointed out that the capital cities have manifested greater attention to ideological themes than have other areas. In a political system in which the parties have relatively little significance as ideological forces, this emphasis was a marked departure from the patronage and personalism that has continued to dominate the political process in the rural areas. In Ceará, Ribeiro writes, "This manifestation of the capital [Fortaleza] was more than a preference of a personal order. It was above all, a taking of a position of an ideological character." [14] Such a finding would seem to be in keeping with some claims that the urban dweller is more concerned about societal goals than is the rural dweller.

However, size alone does not explain voting behavior in the metropolitan areas. Recife and São Paulo showed marked differences in electoral behavior. The campaign of Arrais in Pernambuco appears to have been in keeping with the radical-populist tradition in the state; on the other hand, Jânio Quadros' campaign in São Paulo was much more personal and nonideological. Arrais won a big victory in Recife; Jânio Quadros barely bested the conservative candidate in the city of São Paulo and lost statewide.

The difference in political behavior between Recife and São Paulo has been explained by Jaguaribe as a function of their level of economic development. He relates economic level to political behavior in the following manner:

Economic Form	Political Predisposition
Traditional, Underdeveloped	Patronage, Clientelism
Takeoff stage	Nationalist Progressivism
Developed stage	Liberal Conservatism

According to this scheme, we would expect that the northern part of Brazil still lives in the era of the individualistic political bargain in which a few men of high status and economic dominance hold power.

---

[13] Vamireh Chacon, "Pernambuco," in Cavalcanti and Dubnic, p. 211.
[14] Fávila Ribeiro, "Ceará," in Cavalcanti and Dubnic, p. 90.

Recife, and much of the center-east of Brazil, is said to be in the second category, National Progressivism, which is defined as embracing various forms ranging from socialism to capitalistic progressivism.

São Paulo, and much of the industrial south, is regarded as Liberal Conservative, whose dominant concern is with preserving gains already made:

> They are interested above all, in promoting the maintenance and the development of the institutional system and the productive separation which has provided them with higher and higher levels of life . . . It is important to them to assure the functioning of the mechanism of representative democracy, through which they will maintain the protection of their interests . . .[15]

A comparison of voting patterns in 1962 in the "developed" state of São Paulo and the "takeoff" city of Recife tends to lend some support to the argument that industrialization has brought conservatism to the Paulistas. Whereas the State of São Paulo gave nearly 60 per cent of its votes to conservative or moderate reform candidates, Recife, the only part of Pernambuco said to be at takeoff stage, did almost exactly the opposite, assigning Arrais 62 per cent of its votes.

Within the State of São Paulo, Ferreira made an analysis of the impact of industrialization on voting behavior in the 1962 gubernatorial election.[16] An Industrialization Index, generally similar in concept to that used in this chapter, was employed. Ferreira noted that Jânio Quadros tended to find his greatest strength in the larger industrialized areas. He was, however, weak in the smaller, intensely industrialized communities and in the rural areas. José Bonifacio was strong in the places where Quadros was weak and vice versa. Adhemar de Barros, whose politics have always been difficult to define but perhaps was the most conservative of the candidates, tended to have some strength at all levels. These findings seem to have two implications: (a) it appeared possible for a candidate to bridge the urban-rural, industrial-nonindustrial gap; and (b) there appeared to be a community of interest between the smaller industrial community and the rural areas, rather than a homogeneity of attitude among industrial workers as a whole.

---

[15] Helio Jaguaribe, cited in Chacon ("Pernambuco," in Cavalcanti and Dubnic) without further reference as to original place of publication.

[16] Oliveiros S. Ferreira, "São Paulo," in Cavalcanti and Dubnic, pp. 229ff.

Summary

It has been the purpose of this chapter to explore some of the factors, of a generally urban nature, which are affecting Brazil's political development. Urbanization, conceived in terms of population densities, is one such factor; the scale of urban communities, the work and technological opportunities they provide, and the quality of urban services they are capable of furnishing are other equally significant dimensions.

On the basis of rather fragmentary data, I have sought to show that

1. Urbanization by itself is neither discrete enough nor sufficient to explain political events in a pluralistic country like Brazil.

2. Urbanization and industrialization do not always have a close relationship, though most industrial activity goes on in urban areas. In Brazil some major urban concentrations are developing without a large industrial base; and this development is indicative of the great regional disparities that exist in the country.

3. Levels of industrialization tend to have a high correlation with voter eligibility and voter participation in Brazil. There is not as high a correlation between levels of urbanization and voter eligibility and participation.

4. The scale of the urban areas is assuming increasing significance in the social and political system. The big cities are growing at a rate 30 per cent faster than the urban areas, which are themselves increasing at a rate 24 per cent above the national average; by sheer weight of numbers, the big cities are therefore occupying an increasingly central role in relation to their hinterlands. There is also strong evidence that the big cities tend to have political values markedly to the left of the total society.

CHAPTER THREE

THE MUNICIPALITY IN THE GOVERNMENTAL SYSTEM[1]

As has already been noted, Brazil is distinguished by its simple three-tier system of government, which applies for nearly the entire nation. At the end of 1965 there were 4,120 municipalities which were discharging local service functions in 21 states; only the city-state of Guanabara, among the states, operated without this third tier. Even in such territorial governments as Rondônia, Roraima, and Amapá, municipalities existed.

The second largest state in Brazil, Minas Gerais (see Table 7), possessed the largest number of municipalities, 722. Next in number of municipalities was the nation's biggest state, São Paulo (with 573), and the state ranking third in population, Bahia, was also third in number of municipalities. The size of the local government units varied tremendously; one encompassed more than 110,000 square miles, another less than one mile.[2]

Picture for a moment the character of a fairly typical municipality in Brazil. In its 900 square miles of territory live about 50,000 people, most of whom still reside on farms.[3] The land area of the

---

[1] The preparation of this chapter and later ones was immeasurably aided by the work of Professor Diogo Lordello de Mello, Executive Director of the Brazilian Institute of Municipal Administration, whose various papers contain a gold mine of insight and information about Brazilian local government.

[2] Altamira, in the State of Pará (in the Amazon region) was the largest, and Águas de São Pedro, a hydromineral health station located in the State of São Paulo, the smallest.

[3] "The 1950 general census showed that the typical Brazilian municipality had a population between twenty thousand and fifty thousand inhabitants, while the typical city (there is one city for each municipality) had a population of less than five thousand. These figures seem adequate to express the rural nature of the Brazilian population." Diogo Lordello de Mello, *Local Government and Field Services in Brazil: An Outline* (Brasília: 1961), dittoed, p. 13.

31

TABLE 7. NUMBER OF BRAZILIAN MUNICIPALITIES ACCORDING
TO PHYSIOGRAPHIC REGIONS AND STATES, 1965

	Number of municipalities, 1965	Population, 1965 (estimate)
North	*161*	*3,054,000*
Amapá[a]	5	92,000
Acre	25	187,000
Amazonas	44	843,000
Pará	83	1,802,000
Rondônia[a]	2	97,000
Roraima[a]	2	37,000
Northeast	*1155*	*17,423,000*
Alagôas	96	1,362,000
Ceará	303	3,682,000
Maranhão	128	3,097,000
Paraíba	172	2,177,000
Pernambuco	182	4,536,000
Piauí	121	1,374,000
Rio Grande do Norte	152	1,254,000
Fernando de Noronha[a]	1	2,000
East	*1251*	*28,219,000*
Bahia	336	6,617,000
Espírito Santo	53	1,384,000
Guanabara[b]	1	3,857,000
Minas Gerais	722	10,945,000
Rio de Janeiro	63	4,103,000
Sergipe	76	821,000
South	*1248*	*29,802,000*
Paraná	275	6,024,000
Rio Grande do Sul	203	6,182,000
Santa Catarina	195	2,502,000
São Paulo	573	15,326,000
Center West	*307*	*3,910,000*
Mato Grosso	84	1,189,000
Goiás	222	2,452,000
Federal District	1	250,000[c]

[a] Federal territory.

[b] A city-state, without municipalities.

[c] Unofficial estimates put the Federal District of Brasília's population at about 250,000. Other data are from *Anuário Estatístico do Brasil 1965* (Rio de Janeiro: Instituto Brasileiro de Geografia e Estatística, 1966).

municipality is just about twice that of the largest city, territorially, in the United States; Los Angeles, with 2,700,000 people, covers an area of about 456 square miles. The seat of our typical Brazilian municipality has a population of about 5,000. This community is called a "city" and is regarded as the urban core of the jurisdiction. Dotted over the landscape are other small urban clusters.

Generally speaking, "cities" enjoy no special status; but in about one-fifth of Brazil's municipalities, attempts have been made to deal with their needs by the establishment of another level of government, the district. In the state of Rio Grande do Sul virtually all the municipalities are divided into districts. Typically, the number of districts created is small. A study in the state of Minas Gerais in 1954 showed that almost half the municipalities with districts had only two district units; and over 80 per cent had less than six.[4]

Even with its vast area, it is likely that our typical municipality does not have more than three districts. Each of these has its seat, called the "vila." A 1959 study showed that only about 10 per cent of the municipalities with districts elected the district leader; in almost all cases he was an administrative subordinate of the mayor.[5]

Historical Development of the Municipality

The history of Brazilian local government is generally divided according to the three major phases of Brazil's political development: (1) colonial phase; (2) monarchical phase; and (3) republican phase.

THE COLONIAL PERIOD

The colonial period is significant because it marks the initiation of local government institutions as a part of Brazil's Portuguese heritage. As Orlando Carvalho has pointed out so well, the Portuguese practice of a cultural imperialism, that is, the implantation of their institutions on a very much larger country, has been a continuing problem for Brazil. Carvalho comments:

---

[4] Orlando Carvalho, *A Multiplicação dos Municípios em Minas Gerais* (Rio de Janeiro: Instituto Brasileiro de Administração Municipal, 1957), p. 10.

[5] Instituto Brasileiro de Administração Municipal, *Municípios do Brasil* (Rio de Janeiro: 1960), pp. 40–41.

The municipal institution presupposes the existence of certain social factors, like a nucleus of families, a community of life, experience in common, and the same class interests. The Portuguese town of the early days developed chiefly as a center in which men could carry on labor. The conditions demanded of the inferior classes by the charters were more lenient than those imposed by the elite, and the peasants preferred to take shelter under municipal legislation, depopulating the lands of the large landholders.

In Europe, such elements existed and gave sense to the existence of the municipalities. This municipal institution was perfected and developed when Brazil was discovered and colonized. The Portuguese transplanted the institution, but the new milieu was not ready for it. In Minas Gerais, in 1721, according to Dom Lourenço de Almeida, the first governor in Capitania, almost all the residents of Minas lived in a "bad state." In 1731, there were already many married people, but "it is still far from enough for colonial expansion."

Thus, at the time, families were not organized in Minas Gerais, but the territory of Capitania was already divided into eight municipalities. Lacking was a true social base to give life to the institution.

A similar contradiction affected all institution of public power by the Portuguese in Brazil. The colonizers brought their tested institutions which were well-fitted to a small territory and tried to adapt them to the Brazilian setting, immense territorially and sparse in population . . .[6]

The principal problem which arose from this transplant of Portuguese institutions was the obligation of the municipalities to serve both urban and rural interests. The country was predominantly rural, with no real urban life; and so the imported institutions were amended, as well as they could be, to meet the changed conditions. As Diogo Lordello de Mello has written, these local institutions "became centralized politically and decentralized geographically . . . the Brazilian colonial municipality remained in a somewhat primitive stage as a community and was highly ineffective as a unit of government."[7]

It is significant that during the colonial period some of the seeds of democracy were also sown. This democracy was partly the result of the difficulties of communication; some local autonomy existed simply because central controls were impossible. In addition, the local election of administrative and judicial officers was instituted. As in United States

[6] Carvalho, p. 8; footnotes omitted.
[7] Diogo Lordello de Mello, "The Chief Administrative Officer Plan and Its Applicability to Brazilian Municipalities" (unpublished Master's thesis, University of Southern California, 1954), p. 74.

counties, the use of locally chosen officers to administer centrally determined laws represented a very substantial departure from the monolithic
pattern followed in many other countries. Thus Brazil has never known
the kind of centralization which Great Britain imposed on the bulk of
its colonies.

THE PERIOD OF THE EMPIRE

In 1822 Brazil achieved its independence; and it has often been
said that the distinctly Brazilian phase of municipal development began
at this time. It was, however, a dreary period for the advocate of local
institutions. The Constitution of 1824 gave promise of making the
municipalities a vital sector of the governmental system by providing
that every city and village would have a popularly elected council in
charge of their "economic and municipal government." Further, the
councilman with the greatest number of votes was to be the chairman
of the council, in effect, the mayor.

However, four years later, an implementing law was passed which
greatly reduced the powers of the municipal councils. It declared the
municipal councils purely administrative corporations and made their
acts dependent on the approval of the chief executives of the provinces,
who were in turn appointed by the central government. In 1834 there
was a reaction against centering so much power in the hands of the
provincial chief executives; however, the amendment to the Constitution simply transferred some of the provincial authority from the
executive to the legislature. Six years later, in 1840, the executive once
again gained the upper hand.

Theoretically, the provinces might have acted to strengthen local
institutions; but it seems axiomatic that centralized institutions do not
permit such a development. Instead, the tendency seemed to be to
destroy whatever vestiges of local autonomy remained. The appointed
provincial chief executive was a spokesman for a central government.
Furthermore, in 1835 a law was passed which permitted the appointment of the mayors by the provincial executives. Shortly thereafter,
reports Cavalcanti, this pattern was adopted throughout the country.[8]

Although the Constitution of 1824 marked a hopeful beginning

---

[8] Themistocles Cavalcanti, *Manual da Constituição* (Rio de Janeiro: Zahar
Editores, 1960), p. 100.

for local governments, the general opinion seems to be that the monarchy not only had little interest in the development of local institutions, but also operated to discourage them. The picture of municipal government during the period has been described as one of "obscurity and apathy, even of humiliation . . ."[9]

THE REPUBLICAN PERIOD FROM 1889 TO 1946

With the establishment of the federal system under the Constitution of 1891, there was some improvement in the municipal situation. However, the significant relationship was between the states and the central government. The Constitution declared itself in favor of local autonomy, but the specific arrangements in this regard were left to the individual states. As in the monarchical period, however, the states had little interest in fostering local autonomy; and few of the states, Rio Grande do Sul being the most notable exception, took advantage of the opportunity to build more viable municipalities. The local governments still suffered from a dearth of resources. In 12 of the 20 states, the mayors continued to be appointed by the governor, at least in the capitals and in other critical cities.

The emergence of Getulio Vargas in 1930 and the successful staging of a revolution destroyed what little local autonomy had remained. It is curious that the dictator Vargas came from Rio Grande do Sul, the state where the movement toward municipalization had gone the furthest and where municipal performance was generally considered to be the best. In any case, between 1930 and 1934 Brazil had a unitary regime. All legislative bodies, including the municipal councils, were dissolved. The state governors were appointed by the central government and the mayors in turn by the governors. The pattern adopted resembled quite closely the classic French system.

The first attempt to give the municipalities a partnership role in the governance of Brazil came with the Constitution of 1934. A short-lived document, which succumbed to Vargas' insistence on one-man rule in 1937, the Constitution sought to be more specific about the ways in which the concept of local autonomy was to be implemented. There was to be local election of officials, local organization of services, and specified sources of income.

Vargas' reassumption of full power in 1937 officially returned

---

[9] De Mello, *The Chief Administrative Officer Plan . . .* , p. 76.

Brazil to a unitary system. Generally speaking, the 1937–1945 period has been seen as one in which centralization of power was extreme; Henry Reining, Jr., explains:

> As has been stated in a number of places by the official publicists of the Brazilian government, one of the factors of the Vargas revolution of 1930 was reaction against the extreme decentralization which the republican regime had brought upon Brazil . . . The pendulum has now swung to the other extreme. Both the governor and the legislature of each of states have been done away with, and replaced by a presidentially appointed *interventor* and an advisory council, *Conselho Administrativo,* also presidentially appointed. The municipal officials and assemblies have also been disbanded and replaced by mayors appointed by the interventor.[10]

On the other hand, it has been argued that the 1937–1945 period laid the necessary groundwork for the municipalist advances contained in the 1946 Constitution. Luis Simões Lopes, long-time president of the Brazilian Institute of Municipal Administration (IBAM) and a municipalist whose credentials were of the highest order, was a key figure in the Vargas government and served also as president of a commission for the study of states' affairs. This commission, Reining has reported, played an active role in the supervision of state and local affairs.[11] In addition, it undertook major studies of municipal reform and development.

On October 29, 1945, the Vargas dictatorship came to an end and with it Brazil's experiment with the "New State." About one year after Vargas' overthrow, on September 18, 1946, the new Constitution of Brazil was promulgated. It was the basic law under which Brazil's municipalities were to operate for nearly two decades.

The 1946 Constitution

The 1946 Constitution rejected the Vargas pattern of a unitary state and returned the country to a federal system. It followed the general philosophy of the 1934 Constitution; and once again a three-tier system was instituted. The 1946 Constitution is often called "munici-

---

[10] Henry Reining, Jr., "The Brazilian Programs of Administrative Reform," *American Political Science Review,* 34:546 (June 1945).

[11] Ibid., pp. 546–547.

palist" because of the great attention it gave to the question of local autonomy. As has already been pointed out, the Constitution did not require that municipalities be created. Where they were established, however, the Constitution concerned itself with the role that they would perform. In this relationship it saw the states as the basic givers of power and structure, the federal government as the protector against excess, and the municipalities as the users of power.

It is particularly important to note the ways in which the Constitution sought to provide for decentralization of the political system:

(a) Election of local government officers at the local level.

(b) Freedom to adopt an organization pattern congruent with local needs.

(c) Flexibility in the administration of local services.

(d) Independent sources of revenue, and freedom to spend such monies as are collected.

The wording of Article 28 makes these municipal perquisites quite clear:

The autonomy of the municipalities will be assured:

I. by the election of the mayor and councilmen.
II. by its own administration which concerns its own peculiar interest and especially:
   (a) As to the establishment and collection of the taxes of its competence and the application of this income;
   (b) The organization of local public services.

Although the 1946 Constitution guaranteed to the municipality independence from state intervention and excessive control, it did not announce that the municipalities were equal partners in the system. As Cavalcanti wrote in 1960, "The federation in its classic form represents, before anything else, two classes of interests: the national or federal and the state," and the municipalities are "only the expression of a concession of state power."[12] Indeed, as we shall discover in much greater detail in a later chapter, the state of Guanabara voted against the creation of a municipal level of government in 1963. Under the 1946 Constitution, the municipal governments were rather heavily protected

---

[12] Cavalcanti, p. 101.

against encroachments by the states; but this protection did not mean that they had a constitutional right to exist.

The states have shaped the character of local governments in Brazil as a result of rather specific grants of power: (a) control over the creation of new municipalities; (b) the fixing of areas of jurisdiction; and (c) supervision of performance.

The influence of the states has perhaps been most evident in their capacity to create new municipalities, a subject of such significance to the local government role that we will want to discuss it in more detail later. Here it may be noted that only one state, Rio Grande do Sul, has provided for local charters. Municipalities are created by special legislative act, rather than according to procedural requirements which have been set forth either in the Constitution or in general legislation. Except for three states where separate laws have been enacted for the capital cities, there is no classification of municipalities according to size or other characteristics. All cities must operate in terms of the framework established by the state. Not that this framework is unduly restrictive in many cases, but it does serve to emphasize further the role of the state as power giver.

The 1946 Constitution did not specify what functions should be performed or what powers reserved to the municipality, with the result that jurisdictional lines between the levels of government have been murky, to say the least. While there may have been failures of definition, there is little evidence that the states have been reluctant to assign important missions to the local government. In fact, de Mello has pointed out that the average municipality in Brazil has a range of competence that is as broad as that of the state, with the exception of police and judicial functions.[13] However, neither the federal nor state governments have been freehanded in providing the municipalities with resources sufficient to meet these many responsibilities. De Mello went on to say, "The problem does not consist, then, at the moment at least, in increasing the activities of the municipalities . . . but to assure them, through a rational system of grants and supports and technical assistance, the means to discharge satisfactorily the responsibilities which have been charged to them."[14] A former governor of the State of

[13] Diogo Lordello de Mello, *Problemas Institucionais do Município* (Rio de Janeiro: Instituto Brasileiro de Administração Municipal, 1965), p. 16.
[14] Ibid.

São Paulo, Carvalho Pinto, has said somewhat the same thing, declaring that an "equilibrium" between obligations and resources has never been established among the levels of the Brazilian government.[15] A further infringement on the capability of local governments to carry out obligations has been the tendency in some state constitutions to require that certain services be provided by the municipalities and that specific percentages of local income be allocated for carrying them out.

Formally, the states have had considerable power to supervise local finances; and a municipality's failure to maintain fiscal regularity theoretically provides the states with a reason to intervene in local affairs. In fact, however, the states have not gone beyond the setting of legalistic standards; and responsible people do not remember a single case in which a state intervened in a municipality under these provisions of the 1946 Constitution. The abdication of this responsibility by the states, originally seen as a "factor of prestige" for local governments, has turned into a "source of discredit and lack of confidence" in the municipalities. It has been common, observes de Mello, that ". . . during the entire tenure of a mayor belonging to a particular political faction opposed to the majority of the council, his accounts will be refused without examination . . . On the other hand, it also frequently occurs that mayors who dominate docile councils do not present their accounts."[16]

While the states have constituted the main point of intergovernmental contact for the municipalities, it is also apparent that the two decades under the 1946 Constitution saw an increasing number of direct relations between the municipalities and the federal government. As in the United States, there has been considerable "marbleizing" of a cake that had once showed reasonably distinct layers. While the boundary lines between the levels of government were never as tightly drawn in Brazil as in the United States—and therefore the interventions of the federal government into local governments were far more common—it nevertheless seems clear that one of the effects of the "municipalist" tone of the 1946 Constitution was to provide a legitimacy to more direct contacts between the top and bottom layers. Various grant and

[15] Carlos Alberto A. de Carvalho Pinto, "O Artigo 20 da Constituição Federaleas Capitais," *Revista de Administração Municipal,* 72: 328–343 (September–October 1965).

[16] De Mello, *Problemas Institucionais do Município,* p. 30.

shared-tax programs, some of which started under the Vargas regime and later expanded, have been important vehicles in furthering these relationships. Also, the constantly rising inflation in the decade from 1955 to 1965, which left the municipalities without borrowing capability and therefore tightened the financial vise further, undoubtedly provided the basis for the many direct rescue operations in which the central government increasingly engaged.

The high mark in municipal independence is regarded by some as having occurred in 1961, when a Constitutional amendment was passed which raised the share of federal taxes to be returned to the municipalities. As we shall observe in detail later, the reality of this event proved to be quite different from the promise; for few cities got hard cash from the federal treasury. The fact, however, that such a Constitutional amendment was passed—only the fifth in fifteen years—certainly seemed to emphasize the growing recognition of the role of the municipality in the three-tier system. The amount of money involved was not insignificant; it could have increased total municipal income by 70 per cent. Further, the Constitutional amendment sought to regularize the payment of these amounts, setting the period of the year in which they would be due and specifying that they would be disbursed in one lump sum. Why an amendment to the Constitution could be so markedly ignored tells much about the role of the municipalities in the governmental system; it is a question to which we shall return.

The Postrevolutionary Period

The revolution of April 1, 1964, occurred nearly three years before these words were written, but the full effect of this major political event on Brazilian local government seems to have been slow to emerge. Indeed, the revolutionary government, attending to many critical economic and political problems, very likely had little time to concern itself with institutional arrangements at the municipal level; and a continuity was also implied by the government's official adherence to the municipalist framework of the 1946 Constitution.

A review of the record suggests that the shift toward the center occurred more rapidly and with greater profundity than was generally realized. Two motivations seem to have governed the increasing degree of involvement of the center in local affairs: (a) political necessities, which required the purging of hostile elements at the grass roots and the building of support elements; and (b) economic perspective, which looked toward an integrated thrust in development activity by all levels of government. In a sense, the municipalities have been given new status as administrative instrumentalities under the revolutionary government; but costs have quite obviously been incurred at the political level.

It is possible to divide the post-1964 period of municipal activity into two parts: (a) April 1, 1964, to October 27, 1965, during which time the revolutionary government concerned itself with immediate political problems in certain cities and pursued a broad strategy of reform by amendment to the 1946 Constitution; and (b) October 27, 1965, to the adoption of the 1967 Constitution, when rather sharp curtailments of municipal prerogative seemed to occur.

THE FIRST PERIOD

The overthrow of the regime of João Goulart was bound to be felt throughout the Brazilian political system. Nearly all the leaders of the opposition parties, and most particularly those of the Labor elements, were deprived of their political rights and removed from elective offices. It was therefore inevitable that new faces would appear in leadership roles in certain of the municipalities.

Two case histories reveal the general shape of these leadership changes. In the city of Pôrto Alegre, capital of the state of Rio Grande do Sul, the Labor Party had always been strong, a heritage from Getulio Vargas. Its mayor was, as a consequence, a strong pro-Labor man; he was ousted. Having taken this action, however, the revolutionary government did not move to name a replacement, with the result that the president of the city council succeeded to leadership. Later, the city council decided it did not like its new mayor and sought to replace him by the simple expedient of electing a new president of the legislative body. The courts, however, refused to sanction this highly original procedure; and the first man stayed in office.

The Pôrto Alegre case, where the central government concerned itself only with eliminating potential opponents from office, has probably been the most common one. There have also been instances where the central government has taken a hand in picking the replacement as well. Such was the experience in Belo Horizonte, the capital of the state of Minas Gerais, where the revolution began.

The Belo Horizonte case involves the story of an administratively inept mayor, rather than a potentially dangerous political antagonist. Even during the Goulart Presidency, the financial situation in the city had become impossible and the municipality almost totally disorganized. There were many allegations of corruption, not so much against the mayor himself, as against his friends. In order to secure handouts from the federal establishment, the mayor had continued to support President Goulart and to appear with him at various political meetings. Thus, he was a marked man, primarily because of a virtual breakdown of local government in Belo Horizonte and also because collapse had forced him to maintain his close alliance with the soon-to-be-deposed President.

The governor of the state, Magalhães Pinto, a leader of the revolution, sought to avoid involvement. He much preferred that the central government inherit the blame for the intervention that seemed ultimately necessary. Meanwhile, the central government tried to draw in Governor Pinto by making a loan of a billion cruzeiros to the state for support of municipal activities. In two or three months, however, the funds were exhausted. Belo Horizonte was in tumult. A strike was threatened. Then the President called the governor to Brasília and told him he had to get rid of the mayor. With the collaboration of the Army commander in Belo Horizonte, the governor ordered the president of the city council to call a meeting to impeach the mayor.

But here the problem became even more complicated. Belo Horizonte had a vice-mayor who would be the legal successor. Living in Rio and not involved in the administrative affairs of Belo Horizonte, the vice-mayor was not politically acceptable. He, too, was impeached. The president of the council, next in line, resigned; and ultimately the state secretary of the interior, one of the three civilian leaders of the Minas revolution, was named to the post. The deposed mayor appealed to the courts; but the decision was that the act of removal was revolutionary and therefore not subject to judicial appeal.

The Belo Horizonte case makes it quite clear that at least an informal line of command from President to governor to mayor, aided by the military, did exist in Brazil in the period immediately after the revolution. Yet it seems apparent that the inclination in 1964 was to use such power sparingly; approximately six months were required to remove a notably ineffective official from an urban situation fraught with explosive possibilities. The mayor did not lose his political rights at that time; it was two years later, in the fall elections of 1966, that his campaign for the federal Congress was stopped by the cancellation of these privileges for ten years.

The other aspect of the Belo Horizonte case is that the government did apparently install an effective person as the new leader. He boosted taxes sharply and put the administrative house in order. By the middle of 1966, Belo Horizonte was once again regarded as a clean and effectively functioning city.

One other illustration of the way in which the revolutionary government moved on an *ad hoc* basis to deal with problems confronting the new regime comes from the Amazonas. The problem in this case was the multiplication of municipalities. In the years from 1961 to 1963, this sparsely settled state had seen its legislature approve the creation of 251 new local governments, raising the total of municipalities from 45 to 296. It is a story of ghost towns and corruption (to be discussed later). Suffice it to say here, the central government saw to it that the number of municipalities in Amazonas was reduced to 44. The episode seemed to emphasize once again the central government's insistence that the municipalities become a viable part of the total development enterprise.

In more broadly legal-institutional terms, the revolutionary government was also active during the period to October 1965. One of the most important steps taken, however, began in the last days of the Goulart government. About 15 days before the overthrow, the Brazilian Congress passed, and the President signed, Law No. 4320, which established new budget classifications and procedures for all the levels of government—federal, state, and municipal. While the governments of Brazil had previously functioned under a standard set of rules laid down by decree of Getulio Vargas in 1940, it is nevertheless noteworthy that the central government had the power under the 1946 Constitution to intervene directly in the financial management of the states and the municipalities. That prerogative, however, was clearly stated in Article 5, which permitted the Congress to set the general norms of financial law in the country.

In any event, the new law seemed to have rather significant

psychological importance for the revolutionary government. Reformist in tone and advanced in its budgetary concepts, it tended to stress the administrative responsibilities of the municipalities; and the role of the center in initiating the changes was quite apparent.

The revolutionary government also achieved passage of five amendments to the 1946 Constitution that had relevance to the role and status of the municipalities. The effect of these amendments was to provide for more uniformity throughout the country, thus indirectly emphasizing the pivotal role of the federal government. The first of these, Amendment 10, promulgated on November 9, 1964, was designed to promote rural land reform. Since one way of spurring the breakup of large, unproductive estates was taxation, the power to tax rural lands was withdrawn from the municipalities and lodged in the central government. Under the amendment, however, the central government was obligated to return the monies collected to the local governments. The amounts were relatively small, representing perhaps 2 per cent of total municipal income. Despite the laudable purpose of the move and the return to municipal coffers of collected monies, the fact still remained that a revenue source had been removed from the direct control and administration of the local government.

The drive toward national uniformity and a consequent reduction of state and local flexibility was evident in Constitutional Amendments 13, 14, and 15. They provided for concurrent elections at all levels; standard terms of four years for elected municipal officials; a residence requirement of two years as a condition of candidacy; and a requirement to make declarations of wealth at the beginning and at the end of a term of office. Amendment 15 also restricted the freedom of all public agencies in Brazil to employ persons or contract for goods and services in the last 90 days of the term.

On the other hand, Amendment 12, promulgated on April 9, 1965, seemed to strike a blow for municipal autonomy. It removed from the 1946 Constitution a provision enabling the governor of a state to appoint the mayor of the capital city. But since the custom was to elect the mayors of capital cities, the amendment had little practical significance. However, it does probably say something about political relationships among the jurisdictions. At the time, the central government was facing some strong and increasingly antagonistic governors—in particular Carlos Lacerda in Guanabara, Adhemar de Barros in São

Paulo, and Magalhães Pinto in Minas Gerais—who had the power to contest central dominance. Thus the strategy of an earlier day of weakening the states and dealing directly with the municipalities could have been a latent objective of the amendment. As the Belo Horizonte case suggests, however, the Army-backed central government probably never felt itself so weak as to have to give serious thought to such subtleties of maneuver.

It is interesting that the primary legal instrument of the revolution, the First Institutional Act, had relatively little effect on the municipalities. The Institutional Act provided for the removal, retirement, and demotion of local government leaders, as also of all other government officials. Any such action, however, required a decree by the state governor, who could act on the basis of a petition from the municipality's mayor. Despite the little attention paid the municipality in the First Institutional Act, in 1965 one mayor wrote in the *Revista de Administração Municipal* that this was the beginning of a new "centralism" which might return the country to the policy of 1824.[17]

THE SECOND PERIOD

The mayor had been quite prophetic, because the Second Institutional Act of October 27, 1965, did signify a substantial change in the relationships among governmental levels in Brazil. That date, therefore, seems appropriate for beginning the second period of municipal activity after the revolution.

Apparently occasioned by major election defeats in gubernatorial races in the key states of Guanabara and Minas Gerais, the Second Institutional Act was a more detailed and lengthier instrument than the first. Two of its 33 articles dealt specifically with municipal matters. One decreed that city councilmen could no longer be paid for their services; another required that financial viability be clearly demonstrated before a new municipality could be created by a state legislature. Other provisions, dealing with the political institutions of the society, inevitably touched the municipalities. Thus the old political parties were eliminated; the President of the Republic was given the right to end the term of office of any elected official and to recess any legislative

---

[17] Wolfgran Junqueira Ferreira, "Aspectos Negativos da Reforma Tributária," *Revista de Administração Municipal,* 73:420 (November–December 1965).

body at any level; and impeached mayors and councilmen, as well as elected officials at other levels, were denied judicial review.

Perhaps the most striking advance in federal power came in complementary, or implementing, decrees designed to carry out the Institutional Act policies. One of these decrees, issued on December 31, 1965, declared that the President of the Republic might fill any vacancies in the position of mayor or vice-mayor. In addition, it was provided that the appointed intervenor might exercise legislative power; this could occur by the President's simple act of recessing the city council, thus leaving the intervenor as the sole person in authority. If an election were not held and the council's term of office ended, the intervenor might find himself possessing total power. Another decree, issued on March 3, 1966, broadened the powers of intervention of the President. He no longer had to wait for a vacancy and could simply decree intervention; his appointee could then exercise the functions of both the mayor and the city council.

A Ministry of Justice official reported that as of November 1966 71 interventions had actually taken place, and 20 others were in process. Of this number, however, 30 occurred in the State of Rio Grande do Sul and were not replacements: that many new municipalities had been created. It is almost impossible to overemphasize the importance of the power of intervention to the evolving intergovernmental relationships of Brazil; for intervention is perhaps the most extreme infringement on autonomy. Its legitimation in post-1964 Brazil must be regarded as a major event in the approximately 65 years of federalism.

The promulgation of a Third Institutional Act on February 7, 1966, also seemed to underscore the speed and direction with which changes in the system occurred. Less than a year earlier, Constitutional Amendment 12 had been passed, allowing the capital cities to elect their own mayors; in early 1966 that position was completely reversed. The central government now said it was vital to the national security to change to the method of appointing the mayors of the capital cities. The governors were again given the power to appoint the city chief executives, subject to confirmation by the legislative assembly. With the departure of some of the central government's most strident opponents from key governorships, there apparently was less concern about the neutralization of the states.

With the advent of Presidential decrees, the Constitutional amendment as a vehicle of reform passed rather quickly from the scene. Yet, in the waning days of 1965, two of the last four amendments to the 1946 Constitution had major significance for the role of the municipality in Brazil. Amendment 16 inserted a new provision that had the effect of establishing the supremacy of state laws over municipal ones. It permitted Congress to establish a legal process by which municipal laws could be declared in conflict with state enactments.

The other amendment, far more profound in its implications, was enacted after more than a year of study and debate. Amendment 18, passed on December 1, 1965, represented a major reform in the taxation system of Brazil. Scheduled to take effect on January 1, 1967, the amendment altered substantially the sources of income of the municipalities; and the general belief was that the local governments would get less of the total pie. Predictions were difficult, however, because there was no experience with a newly devised sales tax. In any case, it was clear that the gains of 1961 had been erased, with the municipal share of the total federal income-tax revenue reduced from 15 per cent to 10 per cent. In addition, the money was not to be subventioned to the municipalities on an equal-share basis.

From the formal legal point of view, the effect of these changes on the municipalities seems fairly evident. They will have fewer authorized sources of income, somewhat less money from the federal and state governments, and a few more strings on the federal money they do get. The right to state or federal money has not put funds in the municipal exchequer; nor have local tax sources always been exploited. Nonetheless, the pulling back from the municipalist direction of the 1961 amendment is further indication of the move toward a more centralized system.

Though it was rather quickly rejected by the government, a Constitution proposed by a committee of five jurists provides some indication of the trend of nation-state-local relations in Brazil. Appointed by President Castelo Branco in April 1966, the committee had the task of reviewing the various Constitutional amendments and decrees and of incorporating them in a new Constitution. The work was completed in August 1966.[18] It was, in a sense, a codification of the

---

[18] The text of the Constitution was informally released to the newspaper, *Correio da Manhã,* in Rio de Janeiro, and published as a section on August 25, 1966.

directions of the revolutionary government; and apparently the basic criticism was that it did not go far enough in these directions.

The 1966 document, though it called the municipalities "administrative units," nevertheless preserved intact the guarantees of autonomy which the 1946 Constitution had initiated. However, concessions to the new trend of uniformity were also evident, particularly in the budget and personnel areas. The treatment of the problem of state intervention in municipal affairs suggested that the basic relationship was to be between the state and central governments. Where the 1946 Constitution declared that states could intervene in local affairs only when the municipality failed to pay its debts, the 1966 proposal stated that intervention could occur on seven different grounds, including a 90-day delay in meeting salary payments.

In the 1967 Constitution, which was adopted in January and took effect on March 15, 1967, the general thrust of the 1966 proposal was retained. From the formal-legal point of view, the new Constitution added up to a substantial reduction in local autonomy. While guarantees remained that the municipality might elect its own officers, collect its own taxes, and organize according to its needs, the 1967 Constitution placed rather severe constraints on municipal autonomy.[19] These limitations began with controls over the establishment of new municipalities, which were to be governed by nationally established standards. Article 14 directs that legislation be passed setting forth population and financial requirements for new cities, as well as the procedures by which the will of the community shall be determined. Although the 1967 Constitution retreated somewhat from the language of the 1966 proposal with regard to intervention by the states, they were still given more ground to move in on the cities than had been the case previously. Any failure on the part of the municipality to meet its financial obligations could result in intervention.

While the autonomy of the municipalities was to be assured through the election of its officers and the organization of its services, even these traditional areas of independence were restricted. In the first place, the state capitals were not given the right to elect their mayor.

---

[19] The Constitution was promulgated by both houses of the Brazilian Congress on January 24, 1967, and was published by the *Diário Oficial* on the same date. *A Nova Constituição do Brasil* (Rio de Janeiro: Gráfica Auriverde, ltda., 1967).

The executives of the principal cities of Brazil were to be appointed by the governor of the state, with the approval of the legislature. Certain other cities, such as spas, were also deprived of the freedom to elect their own leaders. The time at which municipal elections had to be held was also specified. They had to occur two years before the balloting for national and state officers, which was slated for every four years.

Controls were also placed on the legislative bodies of the municipalities. According to Article 16, no city might have a council composed of more than 21 members. Furthermore, only in cities with a population over 100,000 may legislators receive compensation at levels which are to be set by a supplementary national law.

It is in the financial area that the full weight of the 1967 Constitution's impact on local governments is most clearly to be seen. Though the general pattern of taxes followed Amendment 18 to the 1946 Constitution, there was one significant difference. The degree to which the municipality might share in a state-collected sales tax was reduced from 30 to 20 per cent. Furthermore, there was a very clear effort in the 1967 Constitution to use the federal-grant mechanism to force the municipalities into desired patterns of behavior. Paragraph 5 of Article 13, for example, declares that "No aid shall be granted by the federal government to the states or municipalities before they submit to the appropriate federal office a plan outlining the proposed disbursement of the money." The provision for a special incentive fund embracing up to 10 per cent of the federal income and excise taxes collected in a municipality (also contained in Amendment 18) was retained. This money was to be used at the discretion of the central government as a reward to those municipalities which provided for the "coordination of their investment and tax administration programs."

Another consequential feature of the 1967 Constitution was the authorization of the central government to grant exemptions not only from federal levies but from state and municipal ones as well. Previously, the central government had been able to approve exemptions only from taxes within its jurisdiction.

Finally, the budget controls over the local governments by the center were either retained or expanded. As in the past, the 1967 Constitution gave the federal government the power to set the general conditions and terms of budgeting at all levels of government. In addition, it became a Constitutional requirement that all levels of government have both a capital and a current budget. Also, 50 per cent of the grants from the income and excise taxes were required to go to capital investments. Insofar as the current budget was concerned, no more than 50 per cent of its total could be used to pay personnel.

Summary

While the formal-legal statement of the role of the municipality in the governmental system is only one indication of the pattern of relationships, it is interesting to observe how varied has been the manifest doctrine in the roughly 75 years since the founding of the republic.

Prior to the revolution of 1930, the municipality enjoyed little identity and was seen as a subordinate unit of the state government. With the short-lived 1934 Constitution, the municipalities achieved a new recognition, new powers, and new sources of income. However, the period of Vargas' "New State," from 1937 to 1945, seems to have been generally one of centralization. Even so, there is evidence that the national government was preparing to assign more tasks and freedoms to the local governments. The 1946 Constitution legitimated many of these tendencies and was regarded as "municipalist" because of the new status it accorded the local units. Changes in 1961, which provided the municipalities with new sources of revenue, probably represented a high point in local autonomy.

The era of "municipalism" ended with the revolution of 1964. The thrust of the revolutionary government toward a more centralized system began to be apparent with the decree of the Second Institutional Act and with the passage of Amendment 18 to the 1946 Constitution in late 1965. Increased controls were placed over the municipality, and sources of local income were generally reduced. These tendencies culminated in the 1967 Constitution, which took effect on March 15 of that year. While municipal autonomy was officially retained, it seemed quite clear that Brazil had embarked on a new period during which the institutionalization of the grass roots was seen as less important than central control over the political, social, and economic development of the nation.

When the Constitution took effect in March, it was quite apparent that substantial change was in store for Brazil's political units. How durable these changes will be and to what extent they will dig below the formal-legal surface can only be determined by time. Nevertheless, it does seem that one venture in the institutionalization of the grass roots, spurred by the 1934 and 1946 Constitutions, had come to an end. The forthcoming chapters will explore the events and factors that led to the centralizing decisions of the 1967 Constitution.

CHAPTER FOUR

MUNICIPALITIES AS INSTITUTIONS

Institutionalization

It is one thing to ordain a set of relationships among humans; it is quite another for humans to value those relationships for themselves. The 1946 Constitution was a prescriptive instrument. It declared that the municipalities, a rather forgotten segment of Brazilian government, should have new importance, expanded resources, and heightened responsibilities. However, it is a long road between the issuance of the command and its implementation. In this respect, the concept of institutionalization has analytical utility because it forces us to push beyond the mechanistic framework of relationships to the values that either give support or cause disintegration.

Philip Selznick put the matter succinctly when he observed that an organization becomes an institution when it is infused with value:

. . . "to institutionalize" is *to infuse with value* beyond the technical requirements of the task at hand. The prizing of social machinery beyond its technical role is largely a reflection of the unique way in which it fulfills personal or group needs. Whenever individuals become attached to an organization or a way of doing things as persons rather than as technicians, the result is prizing of the device for its own sake.

The test of infusion with value is *expendability*. If an organization is merely an instrument, it will be readily altered or cast aside when a more efficient tool becomes available. Most organizations are thus expendable. When value infusion takes place, however, there is a resistance to change. People feel a sense of personal loss; the "identity" of the group or community seems somehow to be violated; they bow to economic or technological considerations only reluctantly, with regret.[1]

---

[1] Philip Selznick, *Leadership in Administration* (Evanston, Ill., and White Plains, N.Y.: Row, Peterson, 1957), pp. 17–19.

Selznick's remarks provide a series of tests by which we can measure the extent to which Brazil's municipalities have truly become a valued part of the system of governance. Are they, for example, filling personal or community needs to the extent that they have generated profound loyalties? Are they, as a consequence, prized for their own sake? If a new constitution sharply curtailed their powers and functioning, would a substantial body of citizens feel any personal loss?

There are no absolute answers to such questions; and no organization achieves total institutionalization. On the other hand, it is true that the organizational units in any given social system are valued in varying degrees. The national oil monopoly in Brazil, Petrobras, has in a little over a decade achieved a remarkably high degree of institutionalization. It is "untouchable," its extinction unthinkable.

Values are placed on an organization both by its participants and by its environment; and this consideration is particularly important in appraising the degree of institutionalization of Brazil's municipalities. The participants in the organization provide for its essential maintenance. Their ability to make it a creative and adaptive mechanism will determine how it fares in the context of the larger system. A failure to meet the needs of the membership will clearly disturb the necessary equilibrium between rewards and penalties, with a consequent decline in the perceived value of the organization. In the municipal setting, a failure by citizens to make demands on their government, to provide resources, or to participate in the conversion of inputs into outputs leaves the device of government little prized. In a sense, then, what happens in the community cannot help but affect the total system role of the municipality.

Yet it is also apparent that the prizing of local government at the grass roots is mightily influenced by larger events in the governmental system. Certainly, the 1964 revolution represented a substantial change in context; and the degree of institutionalization of Brazil's municipalities will be a function of the desires of the nation's new leaders. A key factor in this picture is the availability of resources. Since the municipalities collect only a small part of the total monies available for public services, they must necessarily look outside their own communities to the larger system for support that will enable them to meet the needs of their membership more fully.

These considerations bear heavily on the degree of autonomy that we may expect the Brazilian municipality to enjoy. If, for example, a municipality is supported largely by its own resources and its jurisdictional boundaries are reasonably specific, it will typically have a high degree of autonomy. This is a simple matter of limits within the system. If a city has high walls around it, grows its own food, and is little dependent on the world outside, intervention by elements of the environment is exceedingly difficult. As the limits become less well defined, it is difficult to establish when organizational autonomy has been violated.

Boundaries need not be physical; indeed, the existence of a strong value commitment to an organization may produce an even more impermeable wall than that which physical boundaries create. Thus, if Brazilians believed that communities *ought* to run their own affairs to the extent that they value the production and refining of Brazilian oil by Brazilians, the municipalities would very likely be "untouchable."

The broader issue of decentralization is, of course, inevitably linked to autonomy. Yet, as the preceding paragraphs have sought to illustrate, autonomy is far more than a legalistic concept. It involves the character of the total social system, the nature of the boundary definitions, the directions and extent of resource flows, and the general level of value commitment to the specified social entity. As a natural consequence, the tests for autonomy, and therefore for degree of institutionalization, tend to be ambiguous. However, a partial listing of the types of factors that seem to represent autonomy may at least serve the function of illustrating the elusiveness of the concept. An organization may be considered to have autonomy when:

1. It originates its own rules and procedures.
2. It aggregates its resources on the basis of values which are widely acknowledged in the social system.
3. It is able to use the values which it represents as devices against intrusion or intervention.
4. It has sufficient control over its environmental relationships to stipulate the sources of its inputs.
5. It has sufficient control over its environmental relationships to stipulate the recipients of its outputs.
6. It has broadly understood boundaries of organizational acceptance.

Katz and Kahn have also emphasized the varied factors that enter into autonomy:

> A fully satisfactory set of theoretical criteria for such assessment [of organizational autonomy] is not available, but it might well include such factors as the following: power to stipulate sources of input rather than accepting sources prescribed by the subsystem; power to choose target populations for export of the organizational product; development of internal mechanisms for organizational regulation, including positive and negative feedback. It may be that many of these criteria will be reflected in a single aspect of organizational life: the ease or difficulty of moving across a boundary. The more difficult such a move and the more extensive the changes which it implies, the greater the degree of organizational autonomy.[2]

In the final analysis, Brazil's system of governance will become decentralized to the extent that its local entities are institutionalized. Institutionalization, in turn, depends on the extent to which the values that the municipalities represent are accepted and shared by the society as a whole. Those who live within the individual municipalities must feel a special stake in, and commitment to, their own unit; and more broadly, the municipalities as a collective body must be prized in the total political system.

Theoretically, we would expect that an institutionalized organization, despite the protection afforded by rather well-defined boundaries, would transact heavily with its environment. Indeed, the filling of needs and the renewal of commitment through new inputs form the essential dynamics of the institution-building process. This process is perhaps most evident at the output level, as Saul Katz has suggested. While an organization must provide the anticipated technical services and products, it must also export to the environment the feeling that these technical outputs *do* meet environmental needs and are to be prized. In ascribing such normativeness to the technical product, the organization as producer is infused with value. Katz calls this composite output an image. "It is this image," he says, "usually of the future, that provides the purpose, goal or output of the system. It may be built around simple

---

[2] Daniel Katz and Robert L. Kahn, *The Social Psychology of Organizations* (New York: John Wiley & Sons, 1966), p. 59.

outputs of commodities or service, but it involves values, norms, and attitudinal and other states of being."[3]

A heavy commerce in outputs raises input questions. Katz and Kahn have pointed out that organizations persist only as long as they can maintain *negatropy;* that is, they must have their own favorable balance of trade.[4] They must import greater amounts of energy than they return to the environment as product. Thus the feedback cycle of systems theory becomes an essential ingredient in the dynamic of institutional development. Prized outputs should trigger new demands and new supports for those demands—the latter in somewhat greater quantity than the energies utilized in the preceding outputs.

The succeeding pages will present the argument that Brazil's municipalities have yet to establish their institutional base fully. In systems terms, their transactions with the environment are relatively limited; outputs have tended to be modest and largely designed to serve the municipalities' political function, and the absence of a dynamic output activity has been reflected in minimal inputs, both in terms of demands and in terms of supports. Such a cycle of events has made it difficult to generate interest and participation in the individual municipal system.

Systems Analysis

Before proceeding further, a brief introduction to systems analysis is in order, for there are about as many ideas on its nature as there are writers and experts. Yet there seems to be little disagreement that the essential purpose of the systems approach is to treat a phenomenon in terms of its totality, rather than its parts. It is also true that the identification of the boundaries of a system always tends to be an arbitrary act, dependent in large part on the purposes of the analysis. This arbitrariness is to be expected because the social and physical world is highly interdependent; any attempt to cut it up into analytically manageable pieces will therefore always encounter difficulties.

The municipality—a formal organization with rather clear territorial boundaries and an established membership—constitutes the basic

---

[3] Saul Katz, *Exploring a Systems Approach to Development Action,* A CAG Occasional Paper (Comparative Administration Group, American Society for Public Administration, 1966), mimeographed, p. 25.

[4] Katz and Kahn, p. 150.

system with which we are concerned. It must be studied in terms of two processes: (a) the ways in which it manages itself so as (b) to cope effectively within its environment. The processes by which energies received are transformed into exported energies provide the reference point for the examination of the operations of the internal system. In this condition of high interdependence, it is assumed that there is a continued push toward equilibrium—between system and environment and within the component, interacting parts of the system.

Gabriel Almond, who, along with David Easton, has probably been the most active proponent of the application of the systems approach to political analysis, has suggested a particularly useful categorization:[5]

> Another way of thinking about the interaction of political systems with their environments is to divide the process into three phases, as is usually done in systems theory—input, conversion, output. The inputs and outputs which involve the political system with other social systems are transactions between the system and its environment; the conversion processes are internal to the political system. When we talk about the sources of inputs and how they enter the political system, and how outputs leave the political system and affect other social systems, we shall in effect be talking about the boundaries of the political system.[6]

Almond lists six types of conversion activity which occur within the political system and which obviously involve the processing of inputs into outputs: (1) receiving interest inputs, (2) assimilating and aggregating such interest demands into policy proposals, (3) making policy proposals into authoritative prescriptions, (4) applying general rules to particular cases, (5) adjudicating the rules in individual cases, and (6) transmitting information about these events.

The Civic Culture, a major empirical study of comparative politics

---

[5] Fred Riggs has commented that Almond's systems formulation is "famous," and he has summed up the model in these terms: "Almond's 'inputs' constitute the group controls over the hierarchy, and his 'outputs,' the hierarchic controls over the population affected." See Riggs, "The Political Context of Administrative Reform: Relearning an Old Lesson," A CAG Occasional Paper, mimeographed, p. 13. Almond's pioneering work, with James Coleman, was *The Politics of the Developing Areas* (Princeton: Princeton University Press, 1960). See also David Easton, *A Framework for Political Analysis* (Englewood Cliffs: Prentice-Hall, 1965).

[6] Gabriel A. Almond, "A Developmental Approach to Political Systems," *World Politics* 17:191 (January 1965).

by Almond and Sidney Verba, relied heavily on systems concepts but added a further analytical dimension.[7] The citizen member of the political community was seen as having two roles, one of an input character and the other as the object of governmental outputs. In the former case the citizen was seen performing *participant* functions; in the latter, *subject* functions. Data on variations in the way these roles were perceived and in particular on the extent of alienation toward them were obtained from five countries (the United States, Britain, West Germany, Italy, and Mexico). It is also interesting that Almond and Verba directed their inquiries toward role expectations at the local government level.

However, it may be observed that concentration on the citizen provides only one type of system perspective. In Brazil, for example, the municipalities *as a whole* form an important subsystem in the national political system. A decision to suboptimize at the municipal level could have highly important political and service consequences for the total society. In a very real sense, our earlier discussion of the legal-formal role of the municipalities was a tacit recognition that they collectively form an important subsystem. This aggregate of municipalities can be called the *national municipal system*. The states and the central government are the significant components in the environment of the national municipal system. Further, it is probable that this relationship can best be understood by focusing on inputs. The amount and types of supports provided seem to tell us most about the extent to which local government outputs are prized and the national municipal system itself is seen as worthy of suboptimization.

A second level of analysis involves the individual municipality. Within this perspective, the attention is directed toward the municipal government itself, which is seen as a subsystem of the community's social and political system. This subsystem may be labelled the *community municipal system*.

In the community municipal system, the role of the citizen is of particular importance. While he clearly is a participant in the system as a voting member of the municipality, the citizen also may be seen as forming its environment. In a real sense, then, he is important for the

---

[7] Gabriel A. Almond and Sidney Verba, *The Civic Culture* (Princeton: Princeton University Press, 1963).

outputs he receives from the municipal government and the inputs he provides. Put in the terms of Almond and Verba, the citizen's role as participant and subject defines an environmental relationship to the community municipal system. Elsewhere, I have used the term "dual-conversion process" to describe the feedback cycle involved. This concept suggests that each citizen forms his own system relationship with a government, in which outputs by the government are received as inputs by the citizen, who acts in his subject role. The citizen processes these inputs into outputs to the government, thus marking his performance as a participant. The outputs of the citizen become inputs to the government, which processes them into outputs; and thus the cycle repeats itself.[8]

In the case of the community municipal system, the three major elements of analysis—inputs, conversion, outputs—all deserve attention. The system can perhaps be best shown graphically:

Diagram 1. The Community Municipal System

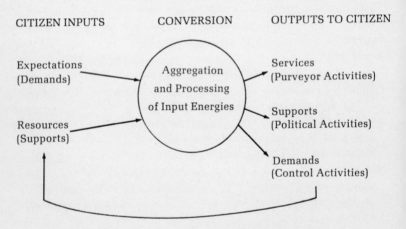

CITIZEN INPUTS   CONVERSION   OUTPUTS TO CITIZEN

Expectations
(Demands)

Aggregation
and Processing
of Input Energies

Services
(Purveyor Activities)

Resources
(Supports)

Supports
(Political Activities)

Demands
(Control Activities)

To summarize, the analytical scheme proposed here involves attention to two systems. The first is the *community municipal system,* in which concern is with the internal processing mechanisms of the municipal government and with relationships to the broader community

[8] Frank Sherwood and Richard W. Gable, *The California System of Governments* (Los Angeles: Dickenson Publishing, forthcoming).

system. The second is the *national municipal system,* which actually functions as a subsystem of Brazil's total political system. Here the municipalities are taken as a collective whole, and the important point of reference is their relationship with the larger political system. As will be explained in greater detail later, this latter relationship can best be understood through an analysis of input supports from the political system to the municipalities.

Boundaries and Municipal Institutions

A system is defined by its boundaries; and therefore the ease with which demarcation points can be identified between the system and its environment is an important first consideration in systems analysis. A restatement of boundaries will result in a redefinition of the system under study.

In the present instance, the analysis of the relationship between boundary and institution is enhanced by the formal-legal manner in which the municipal organization is accorded territorial limits of competence. While such territorial statements do not tell the whole story of municipal boundary conditions, they certainly do establish the size and scale of the individual community municipal system. They also establish the numbers of municipalities in the nation as a whole, a matter of importance to the national municipal system.

Between 1950 and 1964 the state legislatures of Brazil increased the total number of municipalities from 1,761 to 4,114. For the state of Minas Gerais, Professor Orlando Carvalho reported a longer term for increase: at the time of independence in 1822 there were 20 municipalities; in 1863, 65; in 1890, 124; in 1940, 288; and in 1955, 485.[9] By 1964 the number had reached 722. Thus it can be observed that the increase in municipalities in Minas Gerais does not represent a trend of recent origin.

Data from some of the more representative states would suggest that the growth in the number of municipalities has seldom exceeded the rate of urban growth and has often fallen behind that pace. A sample of seven states, presented in Table 8, indicates that only the

---

[9] Orlando M. Carvalho, *A Multiplicação dos Municípios em Minas Gerais* (Rio de Janeiro: Instituto Brasileiro de Administração Municipal, 1957), p. 8.

TABLE 8. INCREASES IN NUMBER OF MUNICIPALITIES AND IN POPULATION
IN SEVEN STATES OF FIVE BRAZILIAN REGIONS, 1950–1960

	Number of municipalities 1950	Number of municipalities 1960	% increase in number of municipalities	% total population increase 1950–60	% urban population increase 1950–60
Bahia (East)	194	338	70	20	52
Minas Gerais (East)	485	718	50	22	53
Santa Catarina (South)	104	177	70	31	66
Amazonas (North)	45	45	0	32	56
Pernambuco (Northeast)	88	102	16	19	47
São Paulo (South)	504	504	0	34	53
Goiás (West)	179	179	0	46	73

Source: Raw data are from *Anuário Estatístico do Brasil 1963* (Rio de Janeiro: Instituto Brasileiro de Geografia e Estatística, 1963). Computations by the author.

state of Bahia had an increase in municipalities substantially above its urban population growth in the decade 1950–1960. Four of the seven states fell measurably behind their urban growth rate.

While these figures suggest that there has been a long-term relationship between the creation of municipalities and urban growth demands, the 1961–1964 period witnessed an unprecedented expansion in the number of municipal units. Fifteen states had an increase from 1962 to 1963; and it was the poorer, northern part of the country where the trend was most apparent. In a single year (1962) the total number in Amazonas rose from 84 to 296, in Acre from 7 to 25, in Ceará from 152 to 302, in Rio Grande do Norte from 113 to 152, in Paraíba from 149 to 163, in Pernambuco from 121 to 182, in Alagoas from 75 to 96, and in Piauí from 102 to 120. Only two of the northern and northeastern states failed to show appreciable increases in the number of municipalities. The trend was far less pronounced in the rest of Brazil, with São Paulo having a net decline, Minas Gerais showing an increase of 4 to a total of 722, and Paraná adding 17 to 260.

The most famous case of municipal explosion was that of the state of Amazonas, which more than tripled the number of its municipalities in twelve months. Technicians of the National Council of Geography made a study of the municipalities created during that period. In general, they discovered that the expansion did not occur in Middle Amazonas, where the demographic density was highest. Rather, the partitioning was in the more depressed and less populated areas. Some of the new municipalities had virtually no people and no community resources. The total population of one unit was a woman and her four children; even the husband was gone most of the time picking tomatoes and other crops.[10] De Mello, writing that Amazonas was the "champion," declared that municipalities were created without a population basis and without defined limits. He continued:

> We saw the locale where one of the municipalities had its seat—an inlet of the River Solimões where the mayor anchored his boat. When the municipality was abolished by the moralizing actions of Governor Arturo Reis, the mayor left with his boat, without leaving any vestige of the municipal seat which the waters of the great river always flood.[11]

Four justifications were given for the increase in the number of municipalities in Amazonas. In the first place, it was said that the old municipalities, some of them larger than many nations in geographical scope, were not capable of contributing to the development thrust. Second, in frontier fashion, there was a need for greater sharing in municipal life. Third, the factor of convenience was noted; it had been necessary to make long trips simply to pay taxes at the municipal seat. Finally, it was emphasized that each of the units would get its share of federal subventions, important to the impoverished residents of the communities involved. However, these arguments did not seem very significant to Governor Arthur Reis, installed by the development-minded revolutionary government. Reis reduced the number of municipalities to 44, one less than had been in existence in 1960.

De Mello has pointed out that most of the 1961–1964 increase in the number of municipalities was legally prohibited. All states, he declares, theoretically operated under the restraint that such changes would occur only every five years. Partly instituted for statistical purposes, this restriction was also designed to observe a Constitutional requirement that judicial boundaries, which are based on the municipality, would not be changed more often than every five years. Why

---

[10] A useful summary of the report of the officials of the National Council of Geography, which was apparently published by the State of Amazonas under the title *Revisão Municipal do Amazonas,* is to be found in *Revista de Administração Municipal,* 77:315–319 (July–August 1966).

[11] Diogo Lordello de Mello, *Problemas Institucionais do Município* (Rio de Janeiro: Instituto Brasileiro de Administração Municipal, 1965), p. 11.

was the law so patently ignored? Apparently the answer lies in two factors, one legal and one financial. The restriction was part of statute law, and state legislators could therefore ignore its provisions as they pleased. The financial factor related to the inflation. Older state laws that imposed economic tests for the establishment of a municipality had been rendered obsolete by the inflation. Thus there was added pressure on the legislators to create special, small municipalities for whom the federal subventions would represent a major source of income.

Whatever the causes and problems, municipal expansion came to a halt with the assumption of power by Castelo Branco. At the end of 1965, there were fewer municipalities in Brazil than existed in 1963, when Amazonas had inflated the total. Only Amazonas, however, experienced a curtailment in the municipalities that had been created.

REASONS FOR MUNICIPAL MULTIPLICATION

Though there seems little indication that Brazil will soon witness another explosion in the number of its municipalities, the 1961–1964 period still occasions interest. The redrawing of boundaries, with the rapid reshaping of old municipalities, was obviously a reaction to certain forces in the environment; and, indeed, the question may be asked whether the tensions that caused such change have been wholly eliminated.

It is significant that most of this activity occurred in the least developed, least urbanized parts of Brazil—the north and the northeast. It is likely that here the concept of the municipality as a local government-service unit was least institutionalized. As a result, there was little reason to prize the old municipal boundaries. Indeed, the abolition of the old institutional lines could bring rewards.

In considerable degree, it was the input factor that provided the push for an expanded number of municipalities in Brazil. The subvention system established by the 1946 Constitution simply gave added impetus to the movement by formalizing the means by which national resources could flow into the local community. Furthermore, the attractiveness of these arrangements was undoubtedly greatest where there was the least expectation that costs would be incurred by the assumption of service responsibilities, as in the north and the northeast. Put another way, the incentive to create a municipality perhaps came less from an expectation and desire for better services and more because a few expected to share in the resources that would be forthcoming.

On the other hand, inadequacies at the conversion and output stages have probably made the old municipal boundaries vulnerable and subject to change. A conversion process that tended to concentrate on the needs of the urban seat of the municipality contributed little to institutionalization; and the generally limited amount of service outputs also probably reduced citizen commitment. The output dimension has been further complicated by the major failure in Brazil to rationalize the respective roles of the three levels of government. In short, very few functional boundaries have been drawn that enable the citizen to link the quality of a particular service with the survival of his local government.

De Mello has written that the government of Brazil has reached a "colossal duplication and sometimes triplication of efforts. . . . The cases are not rare where three services of public health with the same goal function precariously, but simultaneously, in the same city, one municipal, one state, and another federal."[12] He notes that functional boundary problems are particularly to be found in education, rural extension, and public utilities. In each case the municipality would appear to have a basic responsibility; but the states and federal government are as frequently involved. The problem is further complicated in Brazil by a paternalistic budget practice which finds each of the levels of government making substantial contributions to a host of private and semipublic organizations. The effect is a further muddying of the functional boundaries of the municipalities.

The boundary problems of Brazil's local governments would thus seem to have had important institutional effects. For, as we have said, boundaries achieve importance when an organization is institutionalized. Only when an entity is prized do those inside and outside it care enough to raise the question about intrusion or intervention. A very strong local government, toward which many demands and supports flow and which reciprocates with a high level of outputs, is likely to be seen as having not only territorial but also functional areas of dominance and responsibility. With reduced commitment, formal limits are

---

[12] Diogo Lordello de Mello, *Organização do Município* (Rio de Janeiro: Fundação Getulio Vargas, 1965), pp. 21ff.

not only more vulnerable but also more susceptible to change. The 1961–1964 experience in the north and northeast seems to support such a line of argument; output performance was minimal and the input attractions high, and there was very little reluctance to shift the boundaries.

REFORM PROPOSALS

As a result of the changes in the 1961–1964 period, increased attention has been paid to municipal boundary problems. Perhaps the most extreme proposal is that which would take control over boundaries from the states and lodge it in the federal government. Indeed, the proposed Constitution of August 1966 made a start in that direction by requiring that states take into consideration population and finances in decisions on the creation of new municipalities.

In general, the tendency has been to urge the states to toughen the criteria for establishing new units; for the experience in Amazonas demonstrated quite conclusively that land alone cannot make a municipality. Behind the territorial boundaries must be people to function as citizens and as subjects, and resources to finance the enterprise. In its proposals for the constitution of the new State of Acre, the Brazilian Institute of Municipal Administration (IBAM) suggested that a municipality have a minimum of 5,000 inhabitants and that there be at least 50 houses in the community seat. The financial test required that tax receipts amount to at least 10 per cent of the subventions it would have received in the previous year from the federal government.[13]

The same document suggested greater definition of the functional boundaries, particularly that the municipalities assume exclusive responsibilities for a number of the services which are of immediate and local concern. This suggestion was in response to what de Mello has called "the worse possible system of dividing responsibility, the concurrent exercise of power . . ."[14] In seeking to address the issue of more precise functional boundaries, the Acre proposal relied heavily on theories advanced by Benedicto Silva.[15] He proposed that public serv-

---

[13] De Mello, *Organização do Município,* p. 54.
[14] De Mello, *Problemas Institucionais,* p. 16.
[15] Benedicto Silva, *Teoria das Funções Municipais* (Rio de Janeiro: Fundação Getulio Vargas, 1955).

ices be classified in terms of their degree of proximity to the community. Three levels or categories of services were identified: (a) those of immediate importance; (b) those of closely related importance; and (c) those of indirect or intermediate importance. The municipalities would have responsibility for category (a).

From the institution-building perspective, such attempts to establish specific areas of activity and responsibility for the municipalities have important implications. The performance of tasks that are important to the individual's quality of life, such as were proposed for the municipalities of Acre, should leave the organization itself more prized. Also, the assignment of exclusive responsibility could have important effects on the municipality's conversion processes. Unable to charge failures to some other unit of government, the mayor and the council would likely be required to become more oriented toward service outputs.

Summary

This chapter has examined the municipality as an institution, which is an organization whose continuity is highly prized in the society. Autonomy is closely associated with institutionalization because the valued organization must have its own identity, its own boundaries, and its own capability to provide outputs of value to its environment. By definition, then, institutions are essentially autonomous.

The question may be asked whether Brazil's municipalities are indeed institutions. However, the institution-building concept is probably more important as a framework for inquiry than as a methodology for plotting a particular organization on a scale of institutional development. The concepts of systems and institutions share a common analytical focus in that both concentrate on the transactions between an organization and its environment. However, the purpose of the analyses is different. Systems theory tends to concentrate on interdependency and its effect on system equilibrium. Institution theory seeks to establish the degree of value which attaches to an organization in its environment.

Brazil's municipalities can be seen in two systems perspectives: the *national municipal system,* which involves the transactions between the municipalities as a collectivity and the total political system; and the *community municipal system,* which involves the transactions between the municipal government and the community system. In both systems, the municipal government as a formal organization is the base from which the analysis begins.

It is important, therefore, to examine the boundary factors which delimit the municipality in the larger system and endow it with form. The organization as an entity is, in a very real sense, a function of its boundaries. This point of reference has particular interest in Brazil because the period from 1961 to 1964 saw a major increase in the number of municipalities. Territorial boundaries were redrawn and new entities created; and it is suggested that the ease with which these events occurred indicates the small degree of institutionalization that had been achieved by the dismembered municipalities.

Any profound analysis of the factors that lay behind the explosion in the number of local governments raises systemic questions, which have only been alluded to in the preceding pages. The experience in the north and northeast suggests that inputs were seen as ends in themselves; and there was little prizing of the conversion mechanism or the outputs that were produced. In the following chapters, we will want to dwell more intensively on the effects of these attitudes on institutional development.

CHAPTER FIVE

THE COMMUNITY MUNICIPAL SYSTEM: INPUT-OUTPUT FACTORS

The outputs of an organization are the basis upon which it achieves status as an institution. If its outputs are prized, it is likely that the environment will feed back inputs to the organization in the form of further demands and additional supports, most particularly financial resources.

Perhaps one of the greatest difficulties in conceptualizing the role of municipalities in Brazil has been the tendency to link outputs solely to technical services, such as water, roads, sewers, and so forth. In fact, however, the technical product of the municipality is only one part of its obligation; it is also a political unit of consequence. Banfield and Wilson have suggested a dichotomous classification of local government outputs: (a) the *purveyor* activity: supplying goods and service; and (b) the *political* activity: handling local conflict. They comment on their classification in the following terms:

> Since the two functions are performed at the same time by the same set of institutions, they are often concretely indistinguishable. A mayor who intervenes in a dispute about the location of a new public library manages a service at the same time that he settles a conflict but he usually is thought of, and thinks of himself, as doing a single thing—"running the city government." One function may at times be much more conspicuous than the other. In some cities, the service function is decidedly subordinate to the political one . . . In other cities, politics seems to be entirely absent.[1]

Political Outputs

The Banfield and Wilson concept is of particular relevance in Brazil, primarily because it stresses the point that the outputs of the

[1] Edward C. Banfield and James Q. Wilson, *City Politics* (Cambridge: Harvard University Press and the M. I. T. Press, 1963), pp. 18–19.

69

municipality cannot be seen solely in terms of service-type activities. Yet the political function in Brazil differs from that in the United States, where Banfield and Wilson define it as "managing conflict in matters of public importance."[2] Political outputs in the United States, then, are process-oriented. They are less concerned with the allocations and rewards than with the processes by which they are made. Such a preoccupation seems quite appropriate for the mature, democratic society.

In Brazil, on the other hand, the rewards or spoils are seen as the primary outputs. This attitude also is to be expected, for Brazil has been elitist in social structure. Its "coronels" have dominated a largely rural and passive population, for which possession of power has not evoked expectation of responsibility, but an access to privilege.

The municipality is an object of attention because it is the building block of the entire political system. In this respect, it is more akin to the counties in the United States than to the cities; and, where county elections are partisan, the parallel is even closer. It is of particular importance to observe that partisanship has played a unique role in Brazilian political behavior. Party considerations have been the basis upon which many rewards—which would have been given in any case—have been justified. The party has provided the communications channel for people who would probably have had contact anyway. In other words, the parties have played an important formalistic role. They have provided a means by which one could be identified with the winners or the losers, but they have certainly not been important in the choosing of any ideological sides. Furthermore, it would be hard to justify the claim that municipal spoils have contributed materially to the building of national party organizations.

During the period from 1946 to 1964, the pattern tended to be one of individual alignment in which the party affiliation told little about the beliefs of a particular leader or about his relationships to the larger political system. Even the Labor Party (PTB), certainly the most doctrinally consistent of the major units, meant quite a different thing in the state of Bahia and in the state of Guanabara. The Social Democratic Party (PSD), the nation's largest before the revolution and

---

[2] Ibid.

particularly strong in the municipalities, most notably lacked any doc-trinal glue.

Yet the ritualism of the parties is a factor to be considered, a factor which inevitably involves the municipalities. It is instructive, for example, that the abolition of the old parties in 1965 was immediately followed by the creation of two new ones, one progovernment and the other antigovernment. As a result, the relationship between party align-ment and loyalty to the leader was probably clearer in 1966 than it had been in prerevolution days. The National Renovative Alliance (ARENA) was focused on the Presidency and on support of the individual in office, Humberto Castelo Branco. This strengthening of the tie between the party and a national political figure is a further indication of the increasing power acquired by the central government since the 1964 revolution.

In August 1966, the Castelo Branco government issued a decree reinstituting the multiballot-election procedure in most of the nation's municipalities. The thirteen cities with more than 100,000 population in 1960, plus the state capitals, retained the single ballot. The action was generally regarded as a backward step from a much-acclaimed reform that had gone into effect only in 1962, when the government took on the task of printing and distributing ballots at the polls. The old, multiballot system had been widely criticized in the past because it favored the people with money, seemed to add to the possibility of electoral fraud, and favored those in control of the government by providing a built-in vehicle for the distribution of ballots.

Why did the Castelo Branco government, typically reformist in character, take this action? The ostensible reason was that the less literate voter in the rural, interior areas was not able to read well enough to mark a ballot correctly. In a sense, then, a distinction was drawn between the urban and the rural voter. A more likely factor, however, was the formal significance of the party in the political system—implying a need by the government to secure a clear victory in the parliamentary elections of 1966. The multiple ballot was one way of insuring an absolute victory outside the big cities, for the govern-ment had by far the largest resources and was in control of virtually all the governmental units. Predictably, it was the opposition party that was most critical of the return to the multiple ballot. In the elections, the victory of the government was overwhelming and particularly so outside the major population centers.

There are two important facets of the multiple-ballot episode that have a bearing on the municipality as a producer of political outputs. The first of these is that the party, though essentially formalistic, remains an important political mechanism. The municipality provided the infrastructure which made the multiple-ballot system particularly attractive and useful to the governing party.

The second implication involves the urban-rural schism. Both manifestly and covertly, the ballot practice tended to emphasize a difference between urban and rural interest. Literacy was a manifest distinction drawn. The use of the multiple ballots tended to increase the power of the rural municipalities in the state and national political systems, by utilization of a mechanism that assured a vote in favor of the government in power. Returns were far more mixed in the larger cities, thus weakening the influence of urban interests within the government party. It is perhaps fair to say that the rural municipalities again revealed themselves most attuned to political outputs.

Within the community, it seems useful to distinguish among the recipients of the political output: (a) the elite group and (b) the broader membership. What interests the elite group are the more immediate rewards which make it appealing to retain control of the local political system. Jobs, contracts, and privileges either provide gratifications directly or form the basis for indirect income. Since the forms of such political payoff differ from one country to another only in degree, they need not attract further attention here.

There is, however, another way in which elite interests are served. Municipal office is generally regarded as the first step in a political career. Thus control of the local machine provides an important means by which the elite of a community can launch its chosen people toward the higher echelons of the nation's political life. Two of Brazil's most famous recent political figures began their careers in the municipality. Juscelino Kubitschek, President from 1956 to 1961, was first mayor of Belo Horizonte and then Governor of Minas Gerais; and his successor, Jânio Quadros, who made Brazilian history by resigning the Presidency, was a councilman, then mayor of the city of São Paulo. He also served as governor of the state before his sweep to the Presidency in 1960. Challenges to the elite also occur at this level. If a person seeks a political career in Brazil, where the rewards—both psychic and material—tend to be greater than in the United States, he must either conquer the present power holders or accommodate to them. Only in the very large cities does the man on horseback have a chance of building an independent and individual power base.

To put it another way, control at the municipal level generally means access to a political career in Brazil. This type of output function is in particular contrast to the situation in the parts of the United States where local government is nonpartisan. In states like California, it is relatively seldom that a municipal official will move on to partisan political office.[3] The municipal government in such a nonpartisan environment is only one of a variety of means of access to higher political office.

The political outputs for the general membership of the community come in a less direct manner. Nevertheless, they play an important part in shaping expectations toward the community municipal system. As indicated earlier, the autonomy of the average municipality is limited, with the result that getting along with the people in the state capital or in Brasília assumes high priority. Financing arrangements have particularly required this concern. The imperative to provide jobs to the politically faithful has left many a municipality—with a limited financial capability—barely able to pay the salaries of its employed. Nothing is left for the capital improvements and other expenditures that a modernizing society demands. Such additional funds are often critical to the welfare of the community; and they can come only from higher levels of government.

The confused state of intergovernmental relations in Brazil also contributes to the concern about upward influence. Both state and national agencies not only perform many direct services in the local communities, but provide inputs in other ways as well. For example, investment decisions by many of the quasi-independent public enterprises operated by the state and national governments can have great effect on the welfare of a community. In this respect, the situation is

---

[3] A five-year study of mayors in Los Angeles County showed that none had assumed higher political positions. Frank Sherwood and Sherman Wyman, *Role Accoutrements and Relationships of the Municipal Mayor and City Manager* (Los Angeles: University of Southern California, 1966), mimeographed, p. 7.

quite different from that in a developed country, where assurance of return on investment forms the basic constraint on decision makers. For the Brazilian municipality, the investment needs are maddeningly high and the capacity to pay excruciatingly low. Thus the friendly government banker has a special relevance.

In addition, the tradition of the subsidy or subvention to public and quasi-public institutions has been deeply ingrained in Brazil. In 1964, it was said there were 80,000 amendments to the budget bill, most of them proposals for subsidies to an infinite range of activities and organizations operating in the remotest reaches of the land. Although efforts have been made to reduce this array of small payments to all sorts of units, the Castelo Branco government found it very difficult to effect any change. The subsidy is one of the prime forms of political output to the local community. Finally, locational decisions with regard to government field offices are of great concern. The more government jobs there are in a municipality, the greater the likelihood of economic well-being. This is particularly true in the rural areas, where federal pay levels are particularly attractive.

The extent of the benefits that higher levels of government bestow on lower ones will have an obvious bearing on the autonomy of the municipality. In the United States, for example, there is nothing like the subsidy program operating in Brazil; and there is a far greater tendency to assign the responsibility for the direct services of government exclusively to local levels. We do not find both state and the local jurisdictions operating schools in the same community in the United States. Yet this situation can occur in Brazil. Even in the case of locational and investment decisions, higher levels of government play a less important role in the United States. A large private economy provides alternative opportunities for bringing material resources to a community.

The result of these imperatives in the Brazilian environment is to place great pressure on the political leader of a community to exercise influence upward. A positive relationship with the governor and/or the President has been perhaps the most important qualification for a position of community leadership in the eyes of the electorate. A specific result of this citizen attitude can be seen in municipal organization. The political leader occupies a pivotal position, not because of his role in resolving community conflict in the Banfield and Wilson sense, but because of his capacity to influence decisions up above. As a consequence, de Mello has argued that the council-manager form of government would not be applicable to the Brazilian scene because its critical figure, the city manager, is expected to be politically neutral and attuned to the purveyor outputs. De Mello feels that the neutral manager would not be effective in exercising upward influence and thus would fail in what citizens regard as his most important leadership responsibility.[4]

He has written that because of the mayor's political and personal prestige,

. . . he is naturally guided to act as the spokesman for his community in the constant and vital battle fought by the Brazilian municipality for assistance from the state and the federal governments, a leadership which the mayors often exercise as "beggars in the halls of the state capitols," as a writer has put it . . . Political ability seems therefore an essential element upon which the mayor depends in his favor-getting relationships with the political masters of the state—state legislators and the governors. Without it he would certainly make an unsuccessful "beggar" for his community.[5]

Another organizational effect of this emphasis on political outputs should be noted. It involves the relationships between the levels of government. According to the United Nations, Brazil is an example of a dual structure in which both center and locality perform services independently. This system, explains a United Nations report, is of "separateness and conflict rather than unity or cooperation."[6] The difficulty is that a review of the formal organizational relationships does not take into account the intergrative function of political-output expectations, as well as other informal factors. Certainly, the system of Brazilian government from 1946 to 1964 had the potential for great conflict between the levels; but the dependence of the municipalities was such as to make the continuation of battle very unhealthy for the local community. Since 1964, the relatively limited number of formal

---

[4] Diogo Lordello de Mello, "The Chief Administrative Officer Plan and Its Applicability to Brazilian Municipalities," (unpublished Master's thesis, University of Southern California, 1954). See particularly Chapter V. The arguments of the thesis are also to be found in de Mello's *A Moderna Administração Municipal* (Rio de Janeiro: Fundação Getulio Vargas, 1960), Caderno Series No. 46.

[5] Ibid., pp. 140–141.

[6] *Decentralization for National and Local Development* (New York: United Nations Technical Assistance Programme, 1962), p. 10.

changes do not at all convey the degree of informal integration that exists within the system.

Purveyor Outputs

The purveyor function involves the whole range of technical outputs—of both a demand and support nature—for which the municipality has been assigned responsibility. While there is obviously some value in describing these outputs for their own sake, it is of much greater importance to bear in mind the feedback cycle by which the citizen converts the feelings he has about outputs received into inputs to the community municipal system.

When a citizen has not been accustomed to receiving any service outputs, it seems rather unlikely that he will hold any high expectations about a future state of service abundance. On the other hand, where abundant outputs have been provided, the expectation would be one of continued performance. In short, a government that does nothing and is largely irrelevant to the life space of its citizens will probably go on doing nothing and being irrelevant.

Tension, or dissatisfaction, seems to be required for participation. When outputs do not reach expected levels, tensions ought to appear that will later be reflected in inputs. With an absence of tension, we would expect little relevant participation. While much of Brazil is apathetic because there is low expectation and low performance, some of the wealthy suburban communities in the United States arrive at the same apathetic state by a different route. They have high expectations but they also get high performance. The important difference is that the suburban situation is characterized by a potentially volatile activism, the Brazilian by alienation. Confident that he can influence the behavior of his government when the need arises, the American is always a possible participant. The Brazilian possesses no such potential. Where tension in the wealthy suburb might be created by a simple drop in performance levels, the problem in Brazil is primarily one of raising expectations.

Inducing tension in the former situation is far easier than raising expectations in the latter. The failure to collect the rubbish on the scheduled Tuesday is sufficient to produce great dissatisfaction in the United States. On the other hand, there are real difficulties in raising expectation levels in Brazil. This failure is in large part due to the fact that reality and expectation contaminate each other. Most individuals cannot tolerate a very high level of tension, and consequently they tend to adjust their aspirations to reality. If performance is low, we can predict that expectation will not be high either. Not having experienced better governmental performance, Brazilians tend to avoid tension by reducing expectations. A fundamental problem, then, is the development of strategies that will create distance between the reality and the expectation.

Another important aspect of the phenomenon of expectation levels exists. Since Brazil has been an essentially rural society, aspirations tend to be seen in individual terms; and the development of collective aspirations has been slow to appear in the urban areas. Yet it is quite clear that the rural-independent-individualist aspiration must be replaced in the urban community by an expectation for the polity.[7]

FORMAL OUTPUT TASKS

Since the Brazilian states are seen as the givers of power to the local governments, the 1946 federal Constitution did not specify the particular responsibilities of the municipalities. Neither did the Constitution debated in 1966.

In its proposed statute of municipal powers and organization for the new state of Acre, the Brazilian Institute of Municipal Administration (IBAM) identified the following purveyor outputs as of immediate, direct concern to the community and therefore as the exclusive responsibility of the municipal government: public utilities (including water, sewers, public transit, telephone, and street lighting), public markets, slaughterhouses, fire fighting, sanitary inspection and control, refuse collection and disposal, and urbanization, which includes street

---

[7] In a most interesting essay, Banfield and Wilson have studied self-regarding and other-regarding orientations in the United States city. It is interesting that the wealthy, white Anglo-Saxons tend to have internalized the other-regarding value more than the other groups. James Q. Wilson and Edward C. Banfield, "Public Regardingness as a Value Premise in Voting Behavior," *The American Political Science Review* 58:876–887 (December 1964).

construction and maintenance, as well as various other public-works activities.[8]

Generally speaking, the states have tended to assign municipalities responsibility for the following types of tasks:

a. Construction and maintenance of municipal roads and streets.
b. The operation of public utilities and the control of those for which concessions have been granted.
c. The operation of slaughterhouses, public fairs, and markets.
d. City planning and zoning.
e. Supervision of private construction.

It will be noted that these are functions of a local nature. In the case of streets and roads, the concern is primarily with those that are urban. Outside the cities, roads and highways can be municipal, state, or federal; all levels of government are involved in such activities. The case of electrical energy is somewhat similar. The federal and state governments, however, are occupying an increasing role in its production and distribution, prompted by the development of large hydroelectric facilities capable of serving a broad geographic area.

Finally, it may be noted that this description of the functions of Brazilian municipalities omits several that have come to be accepted as unalterably local in the United States. The most apparent is the maintenance of a uniformed police force. In Brazil, police work is a state function. Municipalities can maintain a small force only to provide night guards and to enforce local ordinances with regard to building, sanitation, and taxes. The control of traffic is also a state function. In the few states where the municipalities do participate in the management of traffic problems, they are limited to the allocation of parking zones and such other aspects as are related to traffic engineering. Few municipalities maintain a fire department. In the state capitals this function is usually performed by the state government.

OUTPUT PERFORMANCE

It is one thing to catalogue the purveyor activities in which the cities are expected to engage; it is quite another to measure differences among cities and regions in levels of outputs provided. Though the

---

[8] Diogo Lordello de Mello, *Organização do Município* (Rio de Janeiro: Fundação Getulio Vargas, 1965), pp. 15–16.

measure is crude and assumes that function follows money, about the best index to output performance is the expenditure. In other words, we measure output by asking how many inputs in the form of resources have been provided and used. It would be far better to have quantitative measures of output itself; even in the developed societies, however, few data of this sort are available.

Energy must be imported in order to export it in the form of outputs. The over-all lack of input resources in Brazil's municipalities thus sharply reduces the capability of the municipality to perform purveyor functions. Even in the more prosperous areas of the country, there is the impression that resources are often spread so thin as to leave the municipality incapable of performing any real services. In the relatively affluent state of Paraná, for example, the 1963 budget for a predominantly rural municipality (population 18,000) was only $8500.00—about 47 cents per year per capita; this budget is somewhat low, even for Brazil. A five-state survey of over-all municipal expenditures in the same year showed an average annual outlay of only $2.50 per capita. In contrast, a California municipality with a population of about 18,000 at the time of the 1960 census (Colton, California) reported a 1962 expenditure of $67 per capita only for operating activities, excluding utilities, capital outlay, and debt services. In the United States as a whole, the local governments (city, county, school, and special district) had a general expenditure of about $245 per capita. While comparisons with United States expenditures are not of great importance, they do emphasize the point that Brazilian municipalities have very little to spend on purveyor outputs. This lack of funds may, indeed, explain part of the reason why the political function has achieved such importance.

Analysis of the distribution of expenditures at the municipal level reveals that public utilities command the major share of resource inputs of the Brazilian community municipal system. Outputs provided by these expenditures include water, sewers, telephones, and electricity; and in this respect the Brazilian municipality tends to have a broader range of responsibility than is common in the United States. On the other hand, it is noteworthy that about 25 per cent of the outlays of Brazil's municipal governments (those categorized as general adminis-tration, financial administration, and debt service) do not relate to any specific output. Particularly the money that goes into the general-

TABLE 9. OUTPUT EMPHASES IN BRAZILIAN LOCAL GOVERNMENTS
(AS MEASURED BY 1962 EXPENDITURES)

Expenditures for municipalities[a]	% of total expenditures
Public utilities	39.
General administration	15.3
Miscellaneous services	14.6
Education	8.8
Industrial services	6.2
Financial administration	5.9
Debt service	3.9
Public health	3.4
Public safety and social assistance	2.
Agricultural and economic development	.7

Source: Anuário Estatístico do Brasil 1964 (Rio de Janeiro: Conselho Nacional de Estatística, 1964), p. 372.

[a] All Brazilian municipal expenditures are charged to one of the expenditure categories above.

administration category seems removed from the provision of any purveyor services.

While expenditure profiles in the United States and Brazil suggest some differences in purveyor activity in the two societies, such comparisons have substantial limitations. Tables 9 and 10 for example, compare one unit of Brazilian government, the municipality, with a number of units of local government in the United States. Also, the much lower level of financing of local government in Brazil has caused a great many services to be provided by a higher level of government, thus affecting the output demands in the municipalities. Yet the comparison does suggest substantial differences in output commitments of local governments in Brazil and in the United States. Brazilian municipalities have more responsibility for public-utility functions and less for education, they apparently use a higher proportion of their resources for housekeeping and tax-collection chores, and they are much less involved in street construction and maintenance, public safety, and social welfare.

The vast differences among the various geographical areas of Brazil are reflected in a comparison of purveyor activity by the municipalities. Table 11 provides sample data on some of these variations.

In 1964 the Brazilian Institute of Municipal Administration (IBAM) made an exhaustive survey of the operation and management of 52 locally-run water systems in 12 states. It was revealed that these

TABLE 10. OUTPUT EMPHASES IN UNITED STATES LOCAL
GOVERNMENTS (AS MEASURED BY 1962 EXPENDITURES)

Expenditures for municipalities[a]	% of total expenditures
Education	40.0
Public utilities	10.
Highways	8.0
Fire and police	6.5
Social welfare	5.6
Health and hospitals	4.7
Sewers and sanitation	4.2
Unallocable and other	3.
Debt service	3.
Parks and natural resources	2.8
Housing and urban renewal	2.4
Financial administration	1.2

Source: Census of Governments 1962 (Washington, D.C.: Bureau of the
Census, U.S. Department of Commerce, 1964), Vol. V, pp. 184-185.

[a] The U.S. Census identifies several other categories of local expenditures, but none amount to one per cent of the total.

water systems had been linked to only about two-thirds of their potential clientele and that in only about one-fourth of the cases was there a mechanism for metering the water.[9] The report as a whole found serious failures in the management of the systems.

In the analysis of municipal expenditures among the states, we also discover what a variety in performance there seems to exist. In such an important area as public works, the local governments of Paraíba were spending only about 11 per cent as much as those of São Paulo (according to 1961 data); and over-all, municipal expenditures in Paraíba were only about 15 per cent of those in São Paulo. (See Table 12.)

Casual observation tends to support the statistical data. Even in the larger urban centers, one can see evidence of individual effort to cope with problems which in many other societies are treated collectively. Perhaps the best illustration is in water supply. Virtually every home has its own water reservoir, that is, cistern; and in the apartment situation, it often takes up highly valuable space. Frequently, the cistern is the first and most pridefully exhibited feature of one's apartment.

[9] Zadir Castelo Branco, "A 'Realidade Brasileira' em têrmos de Abastecimento de Água," *Revista de Administração Municipal,* 64:204 (May–June 1964).

TABLE 11. QUANTIFIABLE DIFFERENCES IN SERVICE LEVELS
IN A SIX-STATE SAMPLE IN BRAZIL, 1961

	Bahia	São Paulo	Pernambuco	Santa Catarina	Paraíba	Rio de Janeiro
Water Supply; per cent installed in municipalities	33	53	48	21	24	99
Sewer System; per cent installed in municipalities	25	57	26	62	17	16
Telephones; number of persons per telephone	428	30	517	214	673	68
Electricity; capacity in kilowatt hours per person	.065	.17	.012	.046	.007	.27
Hospitals; number of persons per bed	700	290	500	227	420	310

Source: Data have been developed from *Anuário Estatístico do Brasil 1963* (Rio de Janeiro: Instituto Brasileiro de Geografia e Estatística, 1963).

The greater the size of the cistern, the more proudly it is exhibited. As a result, municipal water systems possess very little reservoir capacity and little pressure. Much electricity is also expended as residents turn on illegal pumps to suck water into their private cisterns.

Such behavior is observable not only at the individual level. Large industries, which in many societies would be the most demanding of effective local services, simply remove themselves from the situation. They provide all their own services—and apparently without great economic disadvantage. One pharmaceutical plant visited had its own water system, own sewage disposal, own electrical generation, own fire protection, own plant-security force, and own bus system. Questions to the manager made it evident that nothing was expected from the municipality, with the *quid pro quo* that nothing was to be given either.

In terms of institution building, the obvious relationship between costs and benefits has special significance. An institution becomes prized by its environment when it is perceived to be meeting environmental needs; and thus does it achieve autonomy. Such self-sufficiency depends most on a steady flow of adequate resources, as well as on

TABLE 12. EXPENDITURES ON SELECTED SERVICES IN A SIX-STATE SAMPLE
IN BRAZIL, 1961 (cruzeiros per capita)[a]

	Bahia	São Paulo	Pernambuco	Rio de Janeiro	Santa Catarina	Paraíba
Public security and social welfare	40	56	13	51	12	9.5
Education	36[b]	250	63[b]	80	74	27[b]
Public health	20	120	18	44	15	19
Public works	166	900	460	330	354	98
Aid to agriculture	3.5	2.5	1	2	7.5	6
Total expenditures	500	2400	857	900	741	353

Source: Anuário Estatístico . . . 1963.

[a] Cruzeiro = approximately .004 U.S. dollar.

[b] States in which the municipalities have primary responsibility for education as measured by the number of schools operated.

demand for the product of the organization. Thus the relationship between output and input becomes crucial to the institution-building process. The failure to achieve significant output levels in the great majority of Brazilian municipalities traps them in a vicious circle, in which failure to produce has its direct effect on capability to produce. New input demands do not ensue from old outputs, nor do the resources necessary to finance them. In the community municipal system, there is little conceptual advantage in separating inputs and outputs. It is the relationship between them that is all-important. Outputs appear to be crucial to the creation of expectations; and expectations in turn are pivotal to the generation of inputs.

Input-Output Relationships in the United States and Brazil

In order to probe the relationship between inputs and outputs in the institution-building process more profoundly, an effort will be made in the succeeding pages to discover differences in attitudes between the United States and Brazil. Since the data were developed for other purposes and therefore have certain limitations, the results reported below are intended only to indicate possible areas for further inquiry.

It should also be noted that the data come from the most heavily

urbanized and most economically affluent areas of the two countries—the Southern California region of the United States and the Rio
de Janeiro region of Brazil.

NATURE OF THE STUDIES AND THEIR SETTINGS

Brazil. On April 21, 1963, an election was held in the city of Rio
de Janeiro to decide whether the recently formed city-state would
create municipal governments. The campaign was, in many respects, a
unique one, and a later chapter will be devoted to its themes and
conduct. Here it may simply be noted that the coming plebiscite was
the incentive for professors and students of the Brazilian School of
Public Administration (EBAP) in Rio de Janeiro to conduct two
studies of citizen attitudes toward the establishment of municipalities
in the new city state.[10] The locales of the two surveys were about as
widely diverse as the densely populated Rio metropolitan community
would permit. The first was conducted in the most isolated, rural
section of the state and focused on the community of Campo Grande.
The second was in the densely populated central district of Botafogo.

The plebiscite formed only the point of reference for these studies.
To a considerable degree, the studies were used to further understanding of the attitudes and feelings of the average citizen in the Brazilian
metropolitan community of Rio de Janeiro.

United States. In recent years the attitude survey has become
common in many analyses of United States metropolitan areas, with the
study in Saint Louis being perhaps the most heavily publicized.[11] For
the purposes of this comparative analysis, however, it was decided to
concentrate on studies in the greater Los Angeles metropolitan area,
which, interpreted broadly, includes about eight million people living
on the Southern California coastline.

Between 1956 and 1959 faculty members of the University of
Southern California's School of Public Administration, functioning in
all but one case under the organizational aegis of the Mangore Corpora-

---

[10] These studies are reported in: Jorge Gustavo, "O Projeto de Pesquisa,"
typescript, 19 pages, n.d.; and in Pombo, Fonseca e Silva, Faria, Lopes, and
Wichrowski, "Pesquisa Realizada no Bairro de Botafogo Face ao Problema do
Plebiscito de 21de Abril de 1963," mimeographed, 27 pages, n.d.

[11] See John C. Bollens, ed., *Exploring the Metropolitan Community* (Berke-
ley and Los Angeles: University of California Press, 1961) for detailed ex-
planations of the methods and survey results of the Saint Louis study.

tion, conducted a total of five attitude surveys in highly diverse parts of the metropolis.[12] Populations in the communities varied between 1,000 and 40,000; one was an elite, exurban community, another was located close to the heart of downtown Los Angeles manufacturing; and all levels of income were represented. Three of the communities surveyed (Paramount, East and South Whittier, and Rancho Santa Fe) were definitely considering the possibility of incorporating as municipalities; and, as a matter of fact, only Rancho Santa Fe continues to have unincorporated status at the time of this writing. One was a resort community (Laguna Beach) which already had municipal status but was concerned about its services. The fourth investigation was actually a four-city survey (Bell, Maywood, Vernon, and Huntington Park). These municipalities, located close to the central core of Los Angeles, were giving consideration to the possibility of forming themselves into one municipal unit. That result, however, did not come to pass.[13]

Many differences between the two metropolitan areas in Brazil and the United States could be identified; but the similarities are also noteworthy. Southern California has not crowded so many people into as small an area as has Guanabara, but both share an unmistakable urban character. The coast between Santa Barbara and San Diego is a virtually unbroken urban settlement. Furthermore, the task of supplying urban services on the grand scale is present in both situations. Water supply and distribution, for example, have presented a paramount problem in both areas.

One of the principal differences between these two great communities is man-made. Whereas the three and one-half million people in the State of Guanabara lead a relatively uncomplicated life under one governmental umbrella, the eight millions in Southern California derive their local services from a host of jurisdictions, each of which is independent of the other. It is not uncommon that a property owner

---

[12] For a generalized picture of the Metropolitan implications of these studies, see William B. Storm and Wallace H. Best, "Public Awareness of Metropolitan Problems: Survey Research Estimates," in Ernest A. Engelbert, ed., *Metropolitan California* (Sacramento: The Governor's Commission on Metropolitan Area Problems, 1961), pp. 42–46. Professors Storm and Best were the principal designers of the studies reported here.

[13] Data on these studies are to be found in Henry Reining, Jr., and Frank P. Sherwood, *Government Alternatives in Paramount, California,* dittoed, 1956, and in Mangore Corporation reports.

will be taxed by as many as 10 different jurisdictions for an equivalent range of local services. Another difference of interest and importance also seems to be man-created—the markedly smaller degree of mobility which appears to characterize the Brazilian urban environment. Whereas the North American tends to move easily and often within the metropolitan area at least, the Brazilian is prone to stay in his own neighborhood or district. Of the approximately 1,200 residents interviewed in the United States studies, only about one-third had lived in the community six years or more. Of the 200 interviewed in Brazil, two-thirds had done so.

These factors of governmental structure and residential permanence would appear to be important in the formation of citizen attitudes. Theoretically the pattern seems to favor the Brazilian, who may have less difficulty in identifying who is to blame when the shoe pinches; his experience in the community and his anticipations of staying there also may make his involvement greater. Furthermore, the Brazilian is required to vote in elections, and most of them do in Guanabara. As a result, 90 per cent of those interviewed in Brazil were registered voters, as contrasted with 60 per cent in the United States communities.

One final point should be noted. While the state of Guanabara is one of the most developed and most urbanized parts of Brazil, the area had suffered rather notoriously as a Federal District under the dominance of the national government. With the election of Carlos Lacerda as governor of the new state in 1960, substantial reforms were achieved. Yet the attitudes developed from the years of inattention to the capital's service needs were hardly to be dispelled quickly. Thus, the state represented an interesting admixture of political and purveyor expectations, in which the situation was further complicated by Lacerda's use of purveyor betterments to enhance his political status. In the last analysis, it is probably fair to say that responses from Guanabara represent neither the extreme political end of the output spectrum, such as in the north and northeast, nor the extreme purveyor end, such as in the State of São Paulo.

ATTITUDES TOWARD SERVICE OUTPUTS

In the surveys, the various respondents were asked to evaluate the level of output performance by their governments; and it is interesting that citizens of both cultures appeared to be generous in such evaluation. The Brazilians were a little more critical, 15 per cent saying services were "poor or very poor." In view of some of the service failures that continue to occur in Rio de Janeiro, the registration of a level of approval almost as high as that in Southern California is to be noted. There is frankly no question about the differences in output performance between the two areas. In 1963 Rio continued to encounter serious water shortages, and electrical energy was sometimes off for 20 of 24 hours.

Furthermore, the Botafogo study indicated that citizens had not had very good luck when they did come in contact with their government. Only 14 per cent of the respondents said that they had ever asked for any assistance; and of this number only one-third believed that their requests had been handled satisfactorily. Nearly one-half said that what they had sought had either not been done or had been handled badly. Asked what they would do if they encountered a problem requiring government involvement, 43 per cent said they simply would not allow themselves to have a problem; 36 per cent said they did not know what they would do; and only 21 per cent indicated they would go to the government.

Respondents in both cultures were asked what they thought were the biggest metropolitan-community problems to be solved. The dominant common problem of both areas was transportation. In the United States it was expressed in concern about traffic control and about street construction and maintenance. In Rio it was couched more in terms of mass transit. But in either case these expressions tended to emphasize that metropolitan areas are complex, interdependent communication systems.

Other felt service needs in Brazil concentrated on utility-type services like water and sewers. While there are areas in Southern California where these utilities present problems, the problem is not as common and does not appear in the surveys. Policing was another problem that appeared strongly in the Botafogo survey, quite in contrast to the situation in most Southern California communities. In the study of the four cities, for example, more than 80 per cent of the respondents registered "satisfaction" with this service.

Parks and recreation appeared as a key concern in the Southern California surveys. The performance of these services was heavily criticized; and the need for improvement seemed to have been given priority second only to transportation problems. This emphasis on parks and recreation suggests a difference in the level of development of the two societies. While Rio has its beautiful beaches in which many people find enjoyment, the fact is that there is virtually no neighborhood recreation. One would look in vain for a public tennis court, for instance. Yet these kinds of problems registered virtually no concern on the part of Rio respondents.

On the whole, the data present further evidence that Brazil's urban communitiy still faces the problem of providing the most essential services, whereas the municipal system in the United States has been able to turn its attention toward the amenities.

INPUT-OUTPUT RELATIONSHIPS

Inputs to a system may come in two basic forms: demands and supports. As we have emphasized, both are inextricably tied to levels of output and to expectations about those levels. Citizens of Botafogo were responding in their subject roles (as receivers of outputs) when 80 per cent of them said they would not go to the government, even if they had a problem that required government help. They were responding in subject terms when only 14 per cent said that they had ever asked for assistance, with only one-third of that small group feeling the problem had been adequately handled. Given these circumstances, we can anticipate that the great majority of these people would generate few demand inputs on their government in performing participant roles. Facts seem to support this anticipation. To a question asking whether the respondent participated in his government, about 80 per cent said they either did not or could not make a judgment on the matter. Thus about the same number who said they have nothing to do with the government as subjects also said they had little to do with it as participants, or as initiators of demands.

A second major category of inputs comes in the form of supports. Though there are saturation limits, we would again assume, as with demand inputs, that the higher the level of outputs the greater will be the tendency to provide resource inputs. In other words, a rough maintenance relationship must be established between energy exported and energy imported. Two questions in the surveys at least partially address this dimension by asking whether the creation of a municipality

TABLE 13. ATTITUDES TOWARD THE EFFECT OF
INCORPORATION ON SERVICES AND TAXES,
LOS ANGELES AND RIO DE JANEIRO

	% of respondents	
	Los Angeles	Rio de Janeiro
Services		
Would improve	52	21
Would not improve	19	68
Don't know	29	11
Taxes		
Would go up	40	70
Would stay same	20	10
Would go down	10	5
Don't know	30	15

will (a) improve the quality of public services and (b) increase the
level of taxes.

Two aspects of Table 13, which reports responses to these two
questions, are particularly noteworthy. The first is that the United States
citizen appears to assume a rough relationship between inputs and
outputs. Fifty-two per cent of the United States respondents expected
that an improvement of services would occur under a municipality, and
40 per cent thought that the improved outputs would cost more.
Seventy per cent of the Brazilians believed taxes would go up under a
municipality while only 21 per cent thought services would improve. It
seems clear that the Brazilians did not expect that heightened inputs
would result in increased service outputs; rather it is likely that they
saw a good share of their inputs being converted into political outputs.
Indeed, the specter of a series of municipal councils, "as rotten as Rio's
have constantly been," undoubtedly haunted many respondents.

At the purely theoretical level, there is evidence that Brazilians do
recognize their need for better services and would expect such performance to cost more money. Respondents in the two countries were asked
to indicate their willingness to pay more taxes for better services. The
responses (see Table 14) reveal that the majority of Brazilians (54%)
would be prepared to provide greater inputs for demonstrably increased
outputs. A majority of United States respondents (55%), on the other
hand, probably reveal the high level of service they already think they
have in expressing unwillingness to pay higher taxes for more services.
In assessing these results, it is particularly important to remember that a

TABLE 14. ATTITUDES TOWARD THE PAYMENT OF HIGHER
TAXES FOR IMPROVED SERVICES, LOS ANGELES AND
RIO DE JANEIRO

	% of respondents	
	Los Angeles	Rio de Janeiro
Willing to pay more	36	54
Not willing	55	35
Don't know	9	16

higher level of services is assumed to follow increased taxes. In the Brazilian reality, most citizens apparently will not make this assumption, except for questionnaire purposes. Here, then, is the irony: On the one hand, Brazilians would pay more taxes for more services; but on the other, they think that relatively few of the taxes they pay would *really* result in increased services. How to break out of such a trap is a basic problem in urban development.

The difficulty of the "breakout" process is further evidenced by the surveys in Guanabara. Governor Lacerda had really pushed to raise the level of resource inputs. In fact, cost-of-living studies showed that public-service costs increased two and one-half times in the 1961–1963 period. In some cases, the increases were far steeper; and water rates, a very evident resource input, went up 100 per cent in one year. Yet there was less awareness than might be expected of the extent of these increases. About one in five said they did not know how great the increases had been; and the other 80 per cent split equally between those who said that the tax increase had been more than 50 per cent during the Lacerda regime and those who said it had been less than 50 per cent.

Even though many Brazilians underestimated the extent of the input demands by Lacerda, they still did not believe that an equilibrium had been established between the new level of inputs and the services provided. They did not think output performance had improved as much as taxes had increased in the previous two years.

ATTITUDES TOWARD THE CONVERSION MECHANISM

As a result of these attitudes, and undoubtedly others as well, the Brazilians demonstrated a marked hostility toward the creation of new units of government. Three-fourths of the respondents did not believe

TABLE 15. ATTITUDES TOWARD MUNICIPALIZATION,
LOS ANGELES AND RIO DE JANEIRO

	% of respondents	
	Los Angeles	Rio de Janeiro
Favor municipalization	30	15
Do not favor	53	75
No attitude	19	5

that a municipal government would be any more effective in converting inputs into outputs than was the state. And, as we have seen, there was an expectation that more inputs would be required.

As Table 15 shows, the United States respondents were also antagonistic to the creation of new governments, but not nearly to the degree found in Brazil. It is particularly noteworthy that nearly every one of the Brazilians had an attitude on this question, whereas one in five of the United States respondents did not. In the election in Guanabara, about 95 per cent of the electors voted against creating municipal governments.

Summary

In appraising the role of the municipality in the Brazilian political system, it is perhaps most important to recognize the extent to which the outputs of the municipality interrelate with and condition its inputs. This interweaving, as I have pointed out, profoundly affects the capabilities of the municipalities to emerge as institutions.

The political function of the community municipal system is closely tied to the national political scheme. Indeed, the effectiveness of a political leader at the local level is evaluated very largely in terms of his ability to secure resources from the state and national governments—in terms of subsidies, direct services from these levels, and supports for various types of private and quasi-public enterprises. In turn, the local elite gains immediate rewards as well as access to a broader political stage; and state and national figures secure at least formalistic support in their efforts to gain or maintain power.

Such political outputs, which differ from the type of conflict resolution posited by Banfield and Wilson, have had great influence on the informal integration of governmental activity in Brazil. In general, the rewards from upper levels in exchange for supports have been more influential in conditioning behavior than the formal charts and constitutions suggest. Thus a common story is once more repeated: it is seldom that things are as a constitution says they shall be. Since the 1964 revolution, the move toward central dominance has been more pronounced; yet the attention given to the municipalities, as evidenced by the return to the multiple ballots, suggests that there is a continuing appreciation of their political importance.

At the strictly service level, the significance to the community municipal system of output performance on inputs is quite clearly evident. Interest in providing inputs to a system, either in terms of demands or supports, depends on the expectation that there will be some output of value. To some extent, political outputs perform this function; but the inputs they elicit are small in terms of citizen participation and in terms of resources. Furthermore, concentration on political outputs may result in a fairly high degree of alienation on the part of the membership. The service output, then, has relevance not just because people need their governments to provide water, maintain the streets, and collect the trash. The feelings about these outputs deeply affect the extent and nature of input response. When a citizen feels there is no possibility of securing performance from the municipality as a purveyor, the probability is that he will have little interest in presenting demands as a participant or in providing material supports.

The comparative study of unfortunately limited survey research in the United States and Brazil suggests the viability of this line of argument. The great majority of the Brazilian respondents were quite sure that a new level of municipal government in Guanabara would raise taxes but only about 20 per cent thought there would be an improvement of services. Asked the same kind of question, more United States respondents thought services would improve than believed taxes would increase. Predictably, a substantially greater share of the United States group was sympathetic to creating a municipal level than were respondents in Guanabara.

CHAPTER SIX

THE CONVERSION MECHANISM IN THE COMMUNITY MUNICIPAL SYSTEM

In systems theory, inputs and outputs occur at the boundaries of the system and thus represent the point of transaction with the environment. The activity of the system is concerned with the transformation of energies received as inputs into energies exported as outputs. Such conversion processes occur within the broad maintenance obligations of the system, which seeks to convert inputs in such a way as to cope with its environment. From the institutional perspective, the skill with which the system processes inputs to outputs determines in large part the extent to which it will be valued by its environment.

The community municipal system is composed of the elected officials and functionaries of the municipal government; and the citizens, in their roles as participants and subjects, comprise a critical part of the environment. As a result, the structure into which inputs flow for conversion must be regarded as a basic point of analysis. It should also be remembered that each citizen has his own conversion mechanism, receiving inputs as a subject and processing them for possible transmission as outputs in the form of supports and demands.

There are countless ways in which the conversion activity of the community municipal system may be approached. Basically, however, the concern is a political one. It involves the problem of choice, in which uncertainty and ambiguity rule. How should an entity structure itself to enhance its coping capability? What types of messages should be received, with what kind of symbolic interpretations? What values shall predominate in the utilization of energies? What type of output image shall be sought? When a system has integrity, and therefore some degree of autonomy in the larger system, these types of essentially political questions must be faced.

In the case of the community municipal systems of Brazil, conversions of input energies have been predominantly oriented toward outputs which I have called political. That is, the municipal governments have used much of their resource capability to maintain control of the system and to support those who seek to secure or maintain such control at higher levels. It has been part of what may be called a "national political strategy."[1] In the urban municipality, however, such values have come under increasing attack. There is growing conflict between the political value and the purveyor value in conversion choices. Where service has achieved ascendancy in the hierarchy of conversion values, a commitment to efficiency as a guiding principle has also occurred. In fact, the two are intertwined. As soon as there is concern for the provision of a service, there is also a preoccupation with maximizing benefits in relationship to their costs.

The effects of these shifts in values in the conversion mechanism are pervasive. Indeed, they affect the mechanism itself; for the patterns required to maintain a reward system for the elite are quite different from those implicit in the service value. In the latter case, the process of choice becomes much less automatic and structured; the pursuit of efficiency goals involves new attention to the administrative apparatus basically responsible for producing desired outputs.

Unfortunately, much of what we would like to know about the conversion mechanism in Brazil's community municipal systems has not yet been studied. Nevertheless, there are materials available that at least suggest the types of dynamics that are likely to operate when a Brazilian municipality is free to make some of its own choices.

The Formal Organization

Though formal tables of organization are often misleading, they do offer a departure point for conversion analysis. Indeed, the commitment to the separation-of-powers principle—a structural notion—has clearly had great effect. Mayors have traditionally been elected, on a partisan basis, to serve as heads of the executive branch of the local government. Councils, ranging somewhat in size, have also been di-

---

[1] The term has been used by the Brazilian sociologist Guerreiro Ramos in referring to the ideas expressed here.

rectly elected to carry on their policy-making functions. This pattern is a particularly familiar one in the big cities of the United States. There is a fundamental difference with Brazil, however, as there are no "weak" mayors there; all are "strong." The reason is relatively simple. All the mayors in Brazil are in complete control of the executive establishment. No other administrative officials, such as controllers, clerks, attorneys, and so forth, are elected by the people; nor are there any boards and commissions of consequence.

Separation of powers seems particularly well suited to conversion values that emphasize political outputs. Whereas the authority pyramid tends to be task and efficiency oriented, separation of powers affords a greater diffusion of power. In pre-1964 days, it was quite common to find the members of the legislative body serving one interest, and the mayor another.

THE MAYOR

As the pivotal man in the community municipal system, the mayor has powers in accord with the traditional features of the separation-of-powers doctrine. In addition to his power to appoint and remove key personnel, he (a) presents and executes the budget; (b) publishes and enforces ordinances; (c) imposes punishments and fines for the violation of municipal ordinances, resolutions, and contracts; and (d) is the legal and official representative of the municipality. He participates in the legislative process in three ways: (a) through the veto power; (b) through the general power to initiate legislation and the exclusive right to propose ordinances dealing with salaries; and (c) through the budget.

Aside from problems of staffing and money, perhaps the most serious constraint on the mayor has been a Constitutional prohibition against reelection. Thus, almost from the day he takes office, the mayor's public support tends to diminish. As he approaches the end of his term, which in the prerevolution period was sometimes five years but is now standardized at four, the mayor becomes very much the lame duck. Not only does the one-term provision operate to the power disadvantage of the mayor, it also causes him to impose severe time restrictions on his conversion behavior. He seldom tends to think in terms of the long run because he will neither be a participant in the action nor a recipient of whatever rewards such accomplishments may entail.

THE COUNCIL

Councilmen, who traditionally have been elected for four-year terms with reelection permitted, have two broad areas of responsibility: (a) the development of policy and (b) review and inspection of the activities of the executive branch.

Legislation by the council is generally required on matters of the following types: (1) taxation; (2) approval of the budget proposed by the mayor; (3) concession of tax exemptions and other fiscal favors, as well as of any privileges; (4) concession of public-utility franchises; (5) approval of agreements and compacts in which the municipality is a part; (6) sale or lease of municipal real property; (7) creation and organization of municipal services; (8) borrowing; (9) position classification and salary scales; (10) basic municipal codes, such as the building code, the sanitary code, and other regulatory ordinances; and (11) adoption of master plans, zoning, and subdivision regulations.

In its responsibility for performing as a check on the executive operations of the mayor, the council's most critical power is the audit and acceptance of the mayor's financial accounts for the year. Refusal to accept the accounts has no great legal significance, but it does have considerable importance as a public-relations matter. Secondly, the council has the power to impeach the mayor. In some states this practice is reasonably common; in others, it is very rare.

The size of the city councils has varied considerably, generally in accord with population. According to a 1959 survey, the modal size of municipal councils in Brazil was between 9 and 12.[2] About 60 per cent of the legislative bodies fell in this category; less than 1 per cent had more than 21 members, which is the maximum permitted under the 1967 Constitution.

The pattern of meetings also varies somewhat according to size of the municipality. In the larger jurisdictions the council meets daily from March through December. In the smaller, more rural units, there are typically three sessions a year lasting ten to thirty days. In the more

---

[2] The Brazilian Institute of Municipal Administration (IBAM) carried out a truly monumental survey in 1959 that covered 96.6 per cent (2,340 of 2,423) of the municipalities then existing. The results were reported in *Municípios do Brasil* (Rio de Janeiro: 1960) and cover data for the year 1958. References to the "1959 Survey" are based on information from this source.

urban municipalities the councils may meet on prescribed days throughout the March-to-December period, with the sessions often occurring in the evening.

Councils typically work through committees, on which the various political parties are represented according to their membership in the council. The most common committees are the executive committee, which is entrusted with the internal administration of the council; the budget and finance committee; the public-works committee; the legislative and justice committee, which is charged with the legal aspects of proposed ordinances; the committee of accounts, concerned with reviewing the financial performance of the executive; the education, public-health, and social-assistance committee; and the agriculture and development committee.

ADMINISTRATIVE ORGANIZATION

Conversion activities do not occur only at high policy levels in a municipal system. They involve the total administrative operation.

In 1966 a major new effort was made to direct the organization structure of the municipalities toward a pattern that would yield higher service outputs. The National Service of Municipalities (SENAM), a federal agency, contracted with the Brazilian Institute of Municipal Administration (IBAM) to prepare a model ordinance for the organization and internal operation of the municipalities. The publication that resulted was sent to all municipalities in the country.[3]

Chart 1, a translation of the recommended pattern of organization, indicates that the mayor of an ideal municipality should have eight key officials. Six would be devoted to the provision of the major services of the government; one would handle the finances of the system; and one would be the staff man.

Of the positions suggested, that of municipal secretary is perhaps of greatest interest. The municipal secretary is the chief of the mayor's cabinet, and his is a position of particular trust and confidence. It is a traditional post at all levels of government; the 1959 survey indicated that over 95 per cent of the municipalities had such a position. In the smaller municipal units, the position may involve a great variety of duties, including responsibility for the budget and for accounting. In

---

[3] Serviço Nacional dos Municípios, *Modêlo de Lei de Organização e Regimento Interno de Prefeitura* (Rio de Janeiro: 1966).

Chart 1. Organization Model for a Brazilian Municipality[a]

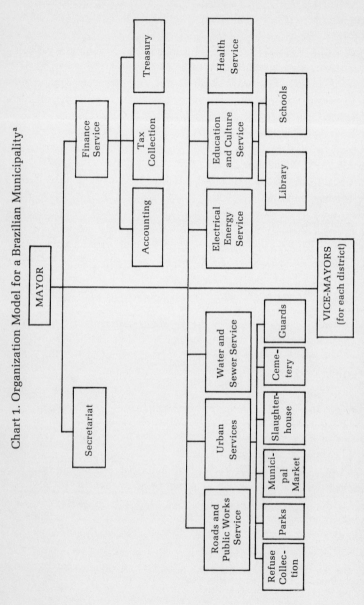

[a]Translated from Serviço Nacional dos Municípios, *Modêlo de Lei de Organização e Regimento Interno de Prefeitura*, p. 72.

the larger units, of course, the secretary of finance assumes these responsibilities.

After the secretary, the next most common administrative figure is the accountant. However, nearly one-third of the municipalities (31.9 per cent) were without such an officer in 1959. Again we see marked discrepancies between the various regions of the country. In the northeast, 84.5 per cent of the municipalities lacked an accounting officer; in the south, over 95 per cent of the local governments had one. As might be expected, the smaller the city, the less likely it was to have such a position.

Lordello de Mello has written that, after the secretary and the accountant, a treasurer-assessor is probably the most common administrative employee. Other typical categories of functionaries are: (1) teachers; (2) storekeepers; (3) fiscal agents in charge of such varied duties as tax collection and assessment, inspection of weights and measures, and enforcement of municipal ordinances and regulations, especially those of a financial nature; (4) public-works chiefs; (5) skilled, semiskilled, and unskilled workers charged with maintenance of public buildings, streets, and cemeteries, operation of the municipal slaughterhouse, and other services; and (6) unskilled laborers for street cleaning, garbage collection, and other such work.[4]

The People in the System

Another means by which to gain insights into the municipal conversion mechanism is through an examination of the characteristics of people who work in the government, the conditions of their participation, and the rewards provided. Such an analysis also provides perspective on the level of institutionalization, for we assume that highly institutionalized organizations not only furnish an adequate level of economic inducements, but also provide normative gratifications.

THE MAYORS

While all mayors are paid, the level of compensation is low in view of the heavy time commitments required. In 1958 more than 75

---

[4] Diogo Lordello de Mello, "The Chief Administrative Officer Plan and Its Applicability to Brazilian Municipalities" (unpublished Master's thesis, University of Southern California, 1954), p. 116.

per cent of the mayors had official salaries of less than $75.00 per month, supplemented by a representation allowance of between $15.00 and $45.00 per month; the income-level distribution follows:

Receive less than $15 per month	6.2%
Receive between $15 and $45 per month	53.0%
Receive between $45 and $75 per month	24.4%
Receive over $75 per month	13.4%
No answer	3.0%

Only 1.3 per cent of the mayors received more than $150 in salary in 1958; and 40 per cent received a representation allowance of less than $15 monthly.[5] With the inflation during the eight years since 1958, it is probable that a similar survey conducted today would show the average mayor in an even less desirable economic situation.

Mayors have a broad variety of backgrounds, as the 1958 study showed. The rural cast of the municipalities is evidenced by the fact that nearly one-third of the mayors were farmers; and the next largest group, retail merchants, was from the urban setting. The background distribution follows:

Farmer	29.0%
Retail merchant	22.4%
Government employee	10.7%
Industrial employee	7.1%
Physician	6.4%
Lawyer	3.3%
Pharmacist	3.1%
Other	18.0%

The strong representation of physicians among mayors is particularly to be noted; for this involvement by medical people in political activity seems quite pronounced at all levels. An analysis of the background of elected representatives in the state of Bahia recently showed that nine of the state's 31 representatives in the national Chamber of Deputies

---

[5] The data reported to IBAM was stated in terms of Brazilian currency. Values in dollars have been computed in terms of foreign exchange rates and provide only an approximate sense of the relationship.

were physicians, as were 12 of 60 members of the State Assembly and 6 of 18 members of the Salvador city council.[6] Some students of Brazilian politics predict that medical men will occupy an even more important political role in the future. The nature of their work puts them in touch with many people in a helping relationship; and they seem to have a desire to hold political office. Former President Kubitschek is a physician.

The age of Brazilian mayors follows a rather normal distribution, the mode being in the 45–49 category. Very few are under 30 or over 70.

In 1966 the Institute of Administration of the University of Rio Grande do Sul made a study of the backgrounds of 30 interventors (appointed mayors) who were taking office in Brazil's southernmost state. The occasion was a special training program developed at the Institute to give the new top officials an introduction to their jobs, which had been created by an expansion of the number of municipalities in the state. Since no elections were being held at the time, the mayors were appointed by the governor with the approval of the President of the Republic.

The group of 30 interventors included only one farmer. Eleven were in retail merchandising, four in industrial activity, seven from civilian government service, and three from the military. Only one was a physician. While the data from Rio Grande do Sul cannot be considered to comprise a representative sample, it is nevertheless tempting to compare this profile with that of the 1959 nationwide survey. The strength of the commercial-industrial representation (about half of the total) is probably reflective of the level of development of Rio Grande do Sul and also of urban growth in the newly established municipalities. The presence of three military people on the Rio Grande do Sul roster, as compared to the absence of an appreciable number in the 1959 survey, is undoubtedly explained by the revolution. The mean ages of the interventors did not differ appreciably from the earlier nationwide sample.[7]

---

[6] Nelson de Souza Sampaio, "Bahia," in Themistocles Cavalcanti and Reisky Dubnic, ed., *Comportamento Eleitoral no Brasil* (Rio de Janeiro: Fundação Getulio Vargas, 1964), p. 55.

[7] Edi Madalena Fracasso, "Seminário de Administração para Interventores Municipais," typescript, 10 pages, n.d.

THE COUNCIL

A continuing debate over compensation for legislators reveals differing perceptions of their function in the conversion process. When the legislative role is seen as extremely part-time and restricted to only the major choices, the chances are that legislators will be expected to serve without pay. Increasing participation suggests greater time requirements and therefore some remuneration. In many of the smaller, nonpartisan, council-manager cities in the United States, for example, service without pay is very common because most of the conversion responsibility is left to the manager.

That compensation has a relationship to role expectation was suggested quite clearly by actions of the postrevolutionary government of Humberto Castelo Branco. In the Second Institutional Act of October 1965, care was taken in Article 10 to deny compensation to all the councilmen of all the municipalities of the country. Since that time, legislators have served without pay and presumably have spent less time on the job, a result the government very likely sought.

The 1959 survey showed that about one-third of the members of city councils were serving gratis; but a more interesting statistic is that a large share of those receiving pay were to be found in the areas where levels of service and presumably demands were least, namely in the north and northeast. While more than half the councilmen in the industrialized south served without compensation in 1959, only 7.9 per cent in the northeast and 11.5 per cent in the north did so.

In general, the compensation for legislative service has been low. The 1959 survey revealed that only about 31 per cent of the legislators received a fixed salary, others being paid by the meeting or in some combination of a small salary and extra pay for meetings. Of those who got a salary, about 60 per cent received less than $11 per month; and only about 1 per cent was paid more than $75 per month.

Expectations about the legislative role express attitudes about the extent to which the municipalities' conversion processes should be responsive to all types of environmental demands. Undoubtedly reflecting his commitment to a vital political process at the local level, de Mello declared in 1961 that service without pay on municipal councils was a "tradition which is now disappearing in Brazil."[8] Time seems to

---

[8] Diogo Lordello de Mello, *Local Government and Field Services in Brazil: An Outline* (Brasília: 1961), dittoed, p. 6.

have proved him wrong in this appraisal. Yet the question still remains whether substantial legislative participation in the conversion mechanism can be achieved without some degree of remuneration.

THE ADMINISTRATIVE ORGANIZATION

It is likely that government service at the municipal level is the least prized of any type of public employment in Brazil. A very limited study of attitudes toward government service at the Brazilian School of Public Administration in 1962, for example, revealed no interest in municipal service. Indeed, students were directing themselves totally toward national government and public enterprises.[9] In a study of about 176 graduates of the same school (approximately 50 per cent of the total), Brandão found only one person employed in a municipality.[10] Another study by Bauzer covering 30 graduates from the years 1954 to 1964 showed none in local government service.[11] A study by Chacon of the attitudes of government officials in the state of Pernambuco revealed that 82 per cent did not want their sons to become municipal employees. Among the local officials he queried, he found none with a college degree and none who had obtained their job by competitive examination.[12]

Low salaries undoubtedly account for much of the disinterest. The 1959 survey showed salaries pitiably poor; and there is little likelihood that they have improved since then, in terms of real buying power. The highest paid municipal official was the engineer, at approximately $61 monthly; next best compensated was the accountant at about $40; and the secretary, treasurer, physician, and lawyer all earned about $30 per month. Schoolteachers were unbelievably badly paid, having an average salary of slightly less than $10 per month. These figures are for salaries only and do not include any extra payments that in many cases account for a 50 per cent increase over these levels. Regional differences are also

---

[9] Frank P. Sherwood, "A Survey of Attitudes Toward Government Service," in Robert Daland, ed., *Perspectives of Brazilian Public Administration* (Rio de Janeiro and Los Angeles: Fundação Getulio Vargas and University of Southern California, 1963), pp. 57ff.

[10] Marina Brandão Machado, *O Ensino de Administração Pública no Brasil* (Rio de Janeiro: Fundação Getulio Vargas, 1966), pp. 42–43.

[11] Riva Bauzer, *Formação para a Administração Pública*, II (Rio de Janeiro: Fundação Getulio Vargas, 1966), Caderno Series No. 63, pp. 115–117.

[12] Vamireh Chacon, "Burocracia e Desenvolvimento," *Boletim do Instituto Joaquim Nabuco de Pesquisas Sociais*, No. 9, 1960, pp. 45ff.

appreciable. Salaries in the northeast were on the whole only about half as high as they were in the south.

But the problem is not salary alone. Chacon's finding that not one of his municipal respondents had taken an examination for his position is particularly revealing. The 1959 survey suggested that there is also very considerable instability in the community municipal system, for only one-third of all employees were regarded by the average municipality as having permanent civil-service status. The rest were probably temporary, daily-rate employees, and were, in most cases, a part of the political reward system. In such a situation it is obviously difficult to expect to develop a conversion process that places high value on service and efficiency.

The Campo Grande Case

In 1958 a wealthy rancher by the name of Wilson Barbosa Martins won election to the chief-executive's post in the municipality of Campo Grande, in the state of Mato Grosso. A candidate of the conservative Democratic National Union (UDN) party, he emphasized the need for reform in the municipality and received support from a number of different elements in the community. Professor L. C. Danin Lobo has written a case study in which he describes some of the problems Mayor Martins encountered in seeking reform in his community.[13] In so doing, Professor Lobo has suggested some of the dynamics involved in the conversion process.

A municipality with a population of over 64,000 in 1960, Campo Grande contained about 11 per cent of the inhabitants of the state; and Professor Lobo reports that "Previous administrations had developed markedly clientelistic policies favoring party factions or pressure groups, increasing or diminishing taxes of each individual according to political criteria." There was, however, a growing urban life in Campo Grande, ". . . which increased the demand for public services and for an efficient municipal administration." In effect, Wilson Martins was the man selected to reshape the conversion mechanism which had been

---

[13] L. C. Danin Lobo, *Estudos de Organização: Dois Casos* (Rio: Fundação Getulio Vargas, 1966), Caderno Series No. 54, pp. 5–72.

oriented toward political outputs into one concerned with service outputs as well.

To undertake his new tasks, the mayor enlisted the support of the Brazilian Institute of Municipal Administration (IBAM), which in turn made arrangements for him to secure the consulting services of a private firm to aid in the implementation of IBAM's recommendations. The Institute's proposals called for major changes in tax policy and administration, in municipal organization, and in the personnel system. Despite the magnitude of the reform, the mayor was in full agreement. The private consulting firm began its work of implementation, which was divided into a legislative and an administrative phase.

The municipal council was a major hurdle. A majority of the nine-man legislative body was opposed to the new mayor. As might be expected, the opposition refused to approve the reform proposals, though one councilman tried to deal with the mayor on the side. He promised to give support to the projects if the mayor accorded him control over municipal patronage. The mayor refused. Through the radio and the press, he took his campaign for approval of the general administrative reform to the people. His effort was successful, and the council finally accepted his proposals.

A second test came with tax reform. Lobo reports that the city was virtually "paralyzed" as businessmen closed their stores in protest. The mayor's own party took a stand against its leader, ". . . for the project contradicted the interests of some members of his own party, who were large retail merchants." The council declared itself in "permanent session" and met daily for one week, starting at 8 a.m. and proceeding on to the following dawn. Tempers were short, the pressure intense, and the insistence great that the "monstrous" tax reform be overturned.

Into this cauldron was pushed the representative of the private consulting firm. One of the top businessmen sought to "demoralize" him by questioning his credentials, by disputing his understanding of the special Campo Grande situation, and finally by quoting the philosopher Kant to prove his points. However, the consultant knew more Kant than did the poor merchant; and he spent two hours proving it. Lobo reports, "There was a definitive silence: no one had the courage to raise objections." The hearing was closed. The next day, however, the undaunted large merchants passed out pamphlets seeking to claim that the increases in taxes would be disastrous for all. The mayor pointed out that only 5 per cent of the taxpayers, who had 80 per cent of the business, were going to feel the burden of the increase. For the others, taxes would be no higher and in some cases lower. The small merchants then came to his support. The tax bill was passed, though it cost the mayor the support of his own party.

Then the administrative phase began. Again, taxes were a major issue. What kinds of output demands were to be made by the municipality on its clientele? The problem, Lobo emphasized, was not just one of setting a policy. How was a "simple functionary" in the "face of the social situation" going to force a large businessman to pay 500,000 cruzeiros where he had paid 10,000 to 15,000 before? Action was taken when a large rancher refused to pay the increased license fees for killing animals in the slaughterhouse. To exert pressure, the rancher staged a "lockout" of meat from the town's refrigerated meat facility, which he owned. The mayor persuaded a retired slaughterhouse operator to go back in business, gave him full support, and was able to bring the big rancher to terms.

Not all the problems involved relationships with the environment. Increased land-tax income, for example, did not founder on taxpayer opposition. Rather, it encountered the problem of records. Ownership and other land information were not complete enough so that demands could be made on the various segments of the environment. Great difficulties were encountered in improving treasury management because the old officeholder found it hard to learn the new methods. Just the opposite occurred in reforming purchasing practices. An official two years from retirement took over the new tasks with great zest. The improvements, Lobo notes, were little short of phenomenal.

Purchase costs were cut in 1960 to about 14 million cruzeiros from about 20 million in 1959, at the same time that four refuse trucks, two trucks, and two jeeps were being added to the municipal fleet. Furthermore, inflation at the time was running about 35 per cent per year, which means that in effect the new purchasing agent cut costs by about two thirds. In 1961 costs finally climbed back to the 1959 figure, despite a 70 per cent inflation. Lobo reports that this was all done "without prejudice to the expansion of municipal services." Lobo provides some explanation for such an amazing performance in noting that the purchasing agent did away with the "ghost services" which were never provided.

The thrust to impose the efficiency value on the conversion mechanism was also seen in the consultants' proposal to hold a civil-service examination for bookkeepers. This proposal caused a "strong impact" in local political circles. The opposition attacked the mayor, declaring that the examination would be nothing more than a farce by which he could appoint members of his own party. Again, the heat was intense. However, resistance was reduced somewhat by appointing eminent people, one a leader of the opposition party, to serve on the examining board. The exams were held, "very capable" people were identified and hired, and the quality of the staff improved.

Yet the gain was not a clear one for the mayor. While Lobo believes that many citizens were impressed by the new merit approach, the mayor's own party, with whom he had tiffed before, was not. It was convinced that the exams had provided an opportunity for opposition elements to secure beachheads in the city hall.

So went the battle to reform the community municipal system and more specifically to modify the patterns and values of the conversion mechanism. Undoubtedly Mayor Martins could look back with a great deal of pride on his accomplishments. But four years go by quickly. It is likely that rather soon many of the values and patterns of the traditional mechanisms reasserted themselves, thus laying the groundwork for a new reform attempt in Campo Grande at some indeterminate date.

A Council Meeting in Resende

This section diverges from the general pattern of the book. What follows is one impression of a city-council meeting in 1963 in a municipality of about 50,000 people. Resende is a three-hour drive from the city of Rio de Janeiro and is located in the state of Rio.

The night was warm when we arrived at the City Hall of Resende, which is best known as the seat of Brazil's West Point. A few people were standing outside the old two-story building, lit dimly by a few globes here and there. A meeting of the city council was supposed to have gotten under way about 30 minutes earlier—at 8 p.m.; but none of the loiterers looked as if they were greatly concerned about what was going on upstairs.

As Professor Jess Swanson and I climbed the stairs, I reflected on the remark our driver had made. We had suggested he get gasoline while we were at the meeting; but he refused. It was too hard to find the city hall—too many "sigee-sagees," as he put it, to take any chances on not discovering his way back. It seemed that the problem of our chauffeur was in some ways typical of Resende. It is a town and yet it isn't. It has significant features and yet it doesn't. The Military Academy, for example, rises in considerable splendor across the river. On the other hand, the town itself has no central point which can be easily identified as the core. One small business section lies adjacent to the Military Academy; the bulk of the commerce takes place across the river near the City Hall.

But, as Professor Swanson has pointed out, Resende is facing an awakening. It lies in the path of considerable industrial development, some of which is already present in the area. In a few years it should be in one of the most favorable situations with regard to electrical energy. The Paraíba River provides an admirable water situation. Good level land is available, and the setting for residential life is very pleasant.

With so much going on in the area, and with the Military Academy almost at door's edge, it seemed hard to believe that the old staircase we were mounting was, indeed, located at the seat of government. Nor did the situation on the lower floor reassure me. One door was securely padlocked from the outside. Inside another room, a man was lounging amid a tremendous amount of old packing boxes and debris of various sorts. Apparently some police operations worked out of the lower floor, but it was hard to imagine how.

As we got to the top of the stairs, we encountered somewhat greater activity. Here we found that the floor was divided into three parts. One wing housed the executive establishment, with a room for the mayor and quarters for the treasury and the legal sections. In the center was the council chamber. The other wing was occupied by the municipal court, which seemed to be in session. As we wandered about the floor, we met the councilman with whom Professor Swanson had had most contact. He was a retired Army major and the leader of the opposition; but he had been defeated for reelection. He was now busy trying to stir up a few more things before he left office in January. As a matter of fact, he had promised us fireworks this evening. He had succeeded earlier in getting the council to refuse to accept the mayor's statement of accounts; and tonight he was going to propose that the matter be taken to the courts. As a result, he was busy mending his fences and preparing for the evening's battle.

It was about 8:45 when we entered the council chamber, with its high ceilings and barren furnishings. About half the room, which was 60 feet in length, had no furniture. There were portraits, in varying states of disrepair, hanging on the walls. The most recent figure I recognized was Getulio Vargas; most of the others had the whiskers and the high collars of the last century. On a table in one corner were the broken remains of an old gilded picture frame, which had been riddled with termites.

About halfway across the middle of the room was a wooden railing, which clearly connoted the separation of the government and the people. On the public side of the railing was one lone bench, which had a seating capacity of five at most. We took our positions there with one other man and woman.

The president of the council was already in his chair at the end of the room. To his left, two chairs away, sat the secretary of the council, a trim attractive young woman of about 30. Two rather lengthy tables extended about 15 feet on the president's right and left. We counted chairs enough for 13 people, including the president. This was curious, in view of the fact that the council had a membership of 15. Since only 12 ultimately appeared for the meeting, we were unable to discover what measures would be taken in moments of a seating crisis. We feared, however, that we might be left standing.

At 8:45 only about six councilmen were in the room. Even for Brazilians, this was a late start for the meeting. By 9:00 it appeared that a quorum would be present, and the secretary began to read the minutes of the last meeting in the dull monotone that seems to characterize such sessions all over the world. This was as close to a formal opening of the meeting as we saw. There was no banging of a gavel, no clearing of the throat and announcement that the meeting was now in order, no recognition of the four lone souls who sat in the audience. Like an old car, the meeting was slowly cranking up.

Several communications were read to the council, and an uneventful discussion took place. Nobody seemed greatly concerned; and, furthermore, it was now time for coffee. As Professor Swanson commented, "No one can say that the Brazilians don't drink their own coffee."

Not too long after 9:00, eleven councilmen were present; and at long last, our friend, the opposition leader, strode into the room to take a seat. He moved a chair, which had sat next to the president's, around and down the side of one of the long tables. He told us he had arrived at the city hall at 7:45. Why had it taken him over an hour to get into the meeting? Where were decisions really being made? At any rate, it now appeared that the session was in full swing.

Members of the council certainly gave no evidence of prosperity. While all but two wore coats, they were typically in rumpled linen. The group was not young. The modal age was probably in the fifties. There were no women among the 12. The president was himself a fairly large, rather portly man; and as the evening wore on, he evidenced real skills in his handling of the meeting. On the president's left were what appeared to be members of the dominant group, the Labor Party, which held seven of the fifteen seats. On the right were members of the opposition, three from the UDN (National Democratic Union), which is a conservative party, and five from the PSD (Social Democrats), which is the party of the center. Nationally, the Laborites and the Social Democrats collaborate, but in Resende, they are at war. Our friend's little UDN block therefore held considerable power as it moved from support of one group to support of the other.

From physical appearances, however, little could be told about party affiliations. The youngest member of the council, perhaps 30, was on the Laborite side. But the older men tended to dominate, two from the Laborites, and two from the opposition, including our friend.

While we were appraising the character of the council, something else was happening. It felt as if the building were in perpetual movement, and I asked Professor Swanson if he had any idea what kind of equipment was causing the building to shake continuously. He pointed to the foot of a councilman at the end of the table. It was bouncing up and down; skillfully, however, so as not to come into full collision with the floor. It seemed inconceivable that one man's foot could move a whole building. Yet the test of observation was there. When his foot stopped for seconds, the movement of the building stopped. One wonders what termite will have the privilege of toppling the city hall.

Suddenly, the drone of the meeting halted. The man with the powerful foot leaped to his feet. He talked so rapidly we could not understand him. But he wasn't happy. He yelled. He demanded. He exorted. There were loud and immediate responses. It looked as if the element most lacking in the meeting was a sergeant at arms. Then, just as quickly, absolute calm was restored. Our man went back to shaking his foot. Others talked to each other, got themselves a glass of water, or just sat in silence.

However, a new issue began to boil. It seemed to develop out of the reading of some materials on the 1963 budget, though we would have to confess that the fast pace of the talk and the lack of an agenda made it hard for us to know exactly what was going on. Yet the issue seemed clear. It involved the limits of the mayor's discretion. Apparently he had spent 12,000 cruzeiros (then about $20) on some item. Somehow, the expenditure had resulted in a gain of 24,000 cruzeiros. It was not clear, though, whether this was a true gain or whether the mayor had found a way to get 24,000, 12,000 of which he spent.

There was an exchange between the UDN leader and the Laborites. Our friend talked calmly but firmly in saying that the mayor had no such rights. A very energetic little man, with a thin wisp of hair on top of his head, took up the defense. His histrionics were quite outstanding. One had the feeling that he was a Brazilian version of Walter Mitty, with a job that kept him in a narrow rut. Explosions on the council were his way of making himself feel important in the society. The exchanges were rapid-fire, with the little man demanding that the UDN opposition make specific charges. "Either it was legal or it wasn't," he said. "Either prove it or shut up," he went on. The UDN man continued on a calm plane, arguing that it wasn't that simple. The little man said, "You're just complaining." "That's right," said the UDN man, "I'm complaining."

There were attempts to introduce other evidence, but the talk kept coming back to the mayor's right to spend the money. Finally, an older man, who was referred to as "professor" and was probably a local teacher, stood up to make a pronouncement. This move seemed significant because none of the others had stood, except the man with the fast foot, who rose in anger. The professor was talking in a soft, deliberate manner. "The UDN is always opposed to whatever is attempted," he said, "but that's all right because it is in the opposition. There are times, though, when this opposition is very dangerous. In this case, the council does not have the right of interference with the mayor . . ."

At this last statement about four members of the council jumped to their feet. It was apparent that nothing quite excites a member of the Resende city council as much as being told he has no rights in the matter.

In the resulting cacophony, we decided to leave. It was nearly 10 p.m. There were as yet no beer bottles, but we had seen plenty of fireworks.

On reflection, there were several factors about the council session that seemed to deserve note. The first was the lack of any public participation. We are certainly used, in the United States, to small public attendance. But in this case not even the press of Resende, which does exist, was present. Obviously, too, no one expected much public participation. There was virtually no place for people to sit. There seemed to be no interest-group representation.

The meeting appeared to have a structure about it; but it was certainly far more informal than the general pattern in the United States. One got no sense of an agenda, though there was a rather clear ordering of events. Whole files were passed around among the council members as the talking went on.

Perhaps most interesting was the general behavior of the council members. They were given a chance to make speeches. Violent differences of opinion were aired. Yet there was a noticeable lack of hostility, except on the part of our man with the fast foot. Serving on the council seemed, in some ways, to be an important prophylactic for a great many repressed emotions. How effective the council was in working as a group, rather than functioning as a debating society, is questionable. Perhaps it is in this respect that the municipal legislative body in the United States differs most from the one in Brazil.

Summary

In the present and preceding chapters, the focus of attention has been on the community municipal system. In this concept the municipal government is considered to have system properties; and the average citizen, though nominally regarded as a participant in local government affairs, is seen as an important part of the environment with which the municipal system must transact.

The environment receives the outputs of the community municipal system, processes them, and generates new inputs to the system. As I have tried to show, any treatment of the environmental context cannot fail to consider the individual conversions by the citizen. Each has his own expectations, each evaluates outputs in terms of these anticipations, and then uses such evaluations to determine the extent to which he will provide inputs in the form of supports and demands. Thus the linkage between output and input is so close that it is literally impossible to talk about one without considering the other.

When an input is received by the community municipal system, the question arises as to what kinds of outputs will be produced; and, in some cases, there is the prior question whether the input will be recognized at all. Then come choices among input demands, priorities to be assigned in the allocation of resource inputs, and decisions about the types of outputs to be produced. Such processing is the essential task of the system.

At this point, a new complexity must be introduced. As we have said elsewhere, systems are always part of larger systems and are essentially creatures of their environment. Thus the conversion of inputs to outputs in a municipal government in Brazil occurs within a broader context of values and expectations in the community and in the society as a whole. The system that endures is the one which accomplishes conversions in such a way as to adapt effectively to its environment by producing outputs that are valued. In the case of the Brazilian municipality, which is urbanizing and therefore experiencing a conflict of expectations, the tension will inevitably be felt in the conversion mechanism.

For example, the separation-of-powers doctrine has seemed remarkably appropriate for a conversion process that has emphasized political outputs. The case of Campo Grande, however, suggests that such a structure may be less applicable to a system in which service and its corollary value, efficiency, compete strongly for input energies. Mayor Martins, limited by a council whose values had not changed, found himself in a slugging match even with members of his own party. Their attitudes very likely were little affected by Mayor Martins' election; nor was there necessarily any change in the ways in which a councilman secured and maintained his power. Indeed, the loss of a patronage appointment or a subvention was probably seen as far more penalizing than a gain in service would be profitable. Only one part of the Campo Grande system was provided with incentives to adjust to the new demands that were apparently coming from the environment.

The case also underscores, in a very simple way, the "open system" relationship of a municipality with its environment. How could a tax collector in a small community bring the top elite to account for failing to pay their taxes?

While it is obvious that conversions are governed by the values that set the criteria for choice, it is nevertheless worth noting, as a final point, that the emergence of the service-efficiency value in the system probably requires a more rigorous, concerted focus on the decision process itself. The quotations from Kant that swung a heated hearing on taxes, as well as the bombastic quality of the Resende council meeting, would have a less important place in systems which are obligated to give tough-minded attention to maximizing at the margins. Indeed, it could be argued that decisions are fairly well programmed in a conversion mechanism geared to political outputs. The rules of the game tend to be well understood, predictable, and generally accepted by all. Such programming seems far less prevalent when conversion decisions place higher value on service-efficiency considerations.

CHAPTER SEVEN

THE NATIONAL MUNICIPAL SYSTEM AND ITS INPUTS

The 1946 Constitution recognized the municipalities as a system in the larger framework of government by providing for their autonomy, by specifying sources of income, and by insisting on their freedom in the managing of the municipal conversion mechanism.

In the United States, in contrast, there has been no Constitutional recognition of a national municipal system. No effort has been made to set boundaries for such a system. Expected outputs are not specified, nor is there any guarantee of resource inputs. If a Constitutional amendment were passed which assigned 5 per cent of the federal income-tax revenue to the nation's municipalities, it might then be said that a national municipal system was being identified.

The emergence of the national municipal system in Brazil is very likely related to the nation's tradition of centralization. Even in the "municipalist" Constitution of 1946, which obviously sought decentralization, the temptation to specify the subsystems of the total political system could not be resisted. Still, specification of a municipal subsystem is a measurable gain over the earlier situation in which grass-roots organization survived only on the whim of higher authorities.

One of the most interesting aspects of this treatment of Brazil's municipalities as a system is the emphasis on inputs from the environment. Very little has been said about outputs. In the 1946 Constitution, resource inputs were very carefully divided among the various levels of government. There was virtually no overlapping. On the other hand, the assignment of output tasks was characterized by almost total ambiguity. Order was supplanted by a commitment to concurrent powers, which has greatly confused the performance of government services in Brazil.

Those who opposed centralization have generally favored the recognition of a national municipal system. Inputs—at least to maintain the system form—have been regarded as critical. While many of the decentralizers undoubtedly hoped that the national municipal system would come to perform important services to the society, regional differences in the nation have made it really quite difficult to specify system obligations. As a result, the central government, either by law or by Constitution, has imposed relatively few specific output demands on the national municipal system. A Constitutional provision, for example, that 50 per cent of the income-tax subventions to the municipalities should go to rural development was apparently never implemented. De Mello noted, in 1965, that the specifics of the requirement had not been defined by the national government in nearly two decades.[1] Shoup has observed that it is not even clear whether half the total municipal spending from this source must go to rural projects or 50 per cent of each municipality's share must be destined to such purposes.[2]

As a result, it seems fairly clear that an analysis of the national municipal system must be made largely in terms of its input relationships with the environment. The inputs to be analyzed are largely of a resource nature. Their analysis tells us what amount of money, under what conditions, Brazil has been prepared to invest in its national municipal system. If the municipalities do represent a cohesive element in the national political system and are therefore valued, we would expect this prizing to be reflected in the way in which money is directed to the municipalities.

At a very gross level, it may be hypothesized that the larger the proportion of resource inputs to local governments, the more they will be prized and the greater their role in the total political system. Paulo Vieira, in a most interesting study of the correlates of decentralization in 45 countries, started from essentially this asumption. He constructed his decentralization indices in terms of (a) the proportion of revenues generated at the local level and (b) the proportion of total expenditures made by the local units.[3]

---

[1] Diogo Lordello de Mello, *Problemas Institucionais do Município* (Rio de Janeiro: Instituto Brasileiro de Administração Municipal, 1965), p. 21.

[2] Carl F. Shoup, *The Tax System of Brazil* (Rio de Janeiro: Fundação Getulio Vargas, 1965), p. 77.

[3] Paulo Reis Vieira, *Toward a Theory of Decentralization: A Comparative View of Forty-Five Countries* (unpublished doctoral dissertation, University of Southern California, 1967).

On this theory, it would have to be concluded that the municipalities of Brazil are not prized highly. İnputs to the municipalities, including transfer payments from higher levels, were a niggardly 8 per cent of total government income in 1962, whereas in the United States local governments received 28 per cent of the total in 1962.

Background of Tax Policy and Practice

Brazilian government has been characterized by a scrupulous definition of taxing power at the various levels of government. This precision was particularly true in the 1946 Constitution, which spelled out in detail the competence of each unit. Shoup described the situation in 1965 in the following manner:

> Brazil became a federal entity by disaggregation rather than by combination, as in the United States of America. Unspecified powers are reserved to the federal government, not the states. The taxing powers of the state, originally nil when they were mere provinces, have grown through adoption of new constitutions and constitutional amendments that have specified precisely what taxes the states may use, and also the taxes available to the municipalities. The taxes that the federal government may employ are likewise named one by one. Any tax not in these lists may be imposed by either the states or the federal government but not by a municipality. The federal government, however, has priority (Article 21 of the Constitution), but at the cost of (1) allowing the states to collect the tax, (2) yielding 40 percent of the revenue to municipalities where the tax is collected and another 40 percent to the collecting state. The mixture of advantages and disadvantages to all concerned has in part kept all states and the federal government from imposing any unspecified tax.
> Complete separation of sources is thus the rule.[4]

Shoup went on to point out that there is little basis for such a rigid separation in public-finance theory. As a result, he called for an "intermediate" system, ". . . allowing a certain degree of overlapping of tax jurisdiction . . ."[5] Shoup's report helped to trigger rather major changes in the tax system, which took effect on January 1, 1967. A fundamental goal was to eliminate the so-called multistage "cascade" sales tax which resulted in the taxation of the same item by different jurisdictions. The new policy has assigned the sales tax specifically to the state and local levels and has left federal sources untouched.

---

[4] Shoup, p. 75–76.
[5] Ibid., p. 77.

In 1964, under the old system, the federal government had a total tax income of CR$ 1,707,615,178,000, of which half, or about 880 billions, came from the excise tax, which is levied at the manufacturing level and is essentially an impost on consumption.[6] According to Shoup, the estimated yield for 1965 was substantially higher, with tobacco and beverage levies accounting for slightly over one-third of the amount.[7] Corporate and personal income taxes yielded about 25 per cent of the total federal taxes. Import levies, stamp taxes (eliminated in the reform), and imposts on combustibles accounted for the remaining quarter.

In the case of the states, data for 1964 show that about 75 per cent of income was from taxes, the rest from service fees and from special grants from the central government. The overwhelming proportion of state taxes (about 90 per cent) was derived from the sales tax. Indeed, this tax accounted for about 68 per cent of all state revenues. Other levies of importance to state financing were the export tax (surprisingly imposed by the states instead of by the central government), the inheritance tax, and the stamp tax.[8]

The income of the municipalities in 1962 was more diversified, with over 35 per cent classified as "extraordinary" or "miscellaneous." About 50 per cent of total municipal revenue was from taxes and another 10 per cent from service charges and fees. De Mello has reported the following percentage breakdown of tax sources: business and industry tax, 42.5%; property tax on buildings and improvements, 27%; real-estate transfer tax, 11.4%; land tax, 9.6%; licenses, 5.5%; taxes on games and amusements, 2.4%; miscellaneous, 1.6%.[9] The real-estate transfer tax was sharply criticized by Shoup because of its high rates, in some cases up to 12 per cent. Such levels, said Shoup, are dangerous economically because they impede transfer of land to its most efficient uses or lead to artificial methods of transfer.[10]

---

[6] Instituto Brasileiro de Geografia e Estatística, *Anuário Estatístico do Brasil—1965* (Rio de Janeiro: 1965), p. 465.

[7] Shoup, pp. 66–67.

[8] *Anuário—1965*, p. 473.

[9] Diogo Lordello de Mello, "A Discriminação de Rendas e o Município," *Revista de Administração Municipal*, 71:257 (July–August 1965). His data are from Conselho Técnico de Economia e Finanças, *Revista de Finanças Públicas*, No. 229 (July–September 1964), p. 31.

[10] Shoup, p. 80.

This profile of tax sources at the various levels has several implications for the national municipal system. First, the situation is much like that in the United States in that the national government makes by far the largest demands for resource inputs on the society; and also the states have come to dominate an extremely important revenue source, the sales tax. Second, Shoup has made a most important point in noting that, for the most part, local taxes are the laggards in responding to Brazil's chronic inflation. Income taxes and excise taxes at the national level and sales taxes at the state echelon are immediately responsive to changes in prices; but property levies, which represented over 35 per cent of municipal income in 1962, are notoriously deficient in this regard.

Of greatest significance is the fact that the total political system imposes extremely rigid constraints on the input potential of the national municipal system. It does this essentially by specifying the kinds of demands for support that can be made at the community-system level. To be sure, a community may maximize within these limitations; but the fact remains that the curbing of such demands has left the national municipal system with comparatively little capability to raise substantial resource inputs relative to the other levels of government. The financial limitations imposed by the total system have therefore made inputs from higher levels more crucial to the maintenance of the national municipal system. De Mello has reported that in about half the nation's municipalities (roughly 2,000) federal subventions from the income and excise taxes account for 70 to 80 per cent of total revenues.[11] Thus, as he has quite rightly reported, any change in the input policy of the federal government would be a "debacle" for the national municipal system.

These constraints obviously have their institutional effects. It will be recalled that an important characteristic of autonomy is the capability and freedom to choose or discriminate among possible inputs from the environment to the system. Theoretically, the greater the freedom a municipality has in making demands on its environment for support, the more total is its autonomy. And, as I have repeatedly noted, such autonomy is tantamount to institutionalization.

---

[11] De Mello, "A Discriminação . . . ," p. 9. In his *Problemas Institucionais*, p. 21, he estimated that the 1965 share for each municipality would be 45 million cruzeiros (about $18,000).

Demand Constraint on the System—to 1964

EARLY DEVELOPMENTS

As Mayor Wolfgran Junqueira Ferreira of the municipality of Estância de Águas do Prata has insightfully written, the struggle to gain revenues for the national municipal system has been "long and arduous."[12] Indeed, it can be properly said that much of the struggle for local autonomy has been waged around the freedom to make resource demands—which is in accord with the broader tradition of governmental development in Brazil. After the deposition of the emperor and the adoption of a federal Constitution in 1891, there was still little independence for the municipalities. At that time, the Constitution makers were careful to spell out the sources of revenue available to the national government and to the states, according to a theory that states should tax factors in the "internal life," such as land, property, and so forth.[13] Nothing was said about the municipalities, indicating that a concept of a national municipal system had not yet achieved importance. Ferreira has commented that the 1891 Constitution represented a trade of "centralism" for "statism," insofar as the municipalities were concerned. He chronicles the fight within the state of São Paulo to secure greater demand capability and reports little success.[14]

It was the federal Constitution of 1934, short-lived though it might have been, that first gave formal recognition to the national municipal system and to the demands it might make. Land and property taxes, licenses, and imposts on games and amusements were made the special revenue sources of the municipalities. Thus, it was "really the Constitution of 1934 that gave financial stability to the municipalities."[15] From that point on, the right to make these demands was rooted in the Brazilian political tradition. Even the centralizing, essentially dictatorial Constitution of 1937 sought no changes; and a 1939 de-

---

[12] Wolfgran Junqueira Ferreira, "Aspectos Negativos da Reforma Tributária," *Revista de Administração Municipal,* 73:414 (November–December 1965). This interesting article has been extremely useful in the preparation of this part of the chapter.

[13] João Camillo de Oliveira Torres, *A Formação do Federalismo no Brasil* (São Paulo: Companhia Editora Nacional, 1961), p. 172.

[14] Ferreira, p. 416.

[15] Ibid., p. 419.

cree law added the freedom to collect fees and charges for services rendered.

THE 1946 CONSTITUTION

With the fall of Getulio Vargas and the reestablishment of democracy in Brazil, the national municipal system gained greater recognition. Inevitably, attention was drawn to ways of providing more inputs to the new, fully recognized tier of government. Much of this attention was directed toward the types of inputs that might be provided by higher levels of government to the national municipal system. Led by Aliomar Baleeiro, now a Supreme Court Justice, efforts were also made to expand the range of demands a municipality might make on its community. As it turned out, the most significant of these new sources was the business and industry tax. Efforts to allow the municipalities to assess property on the basis of highest and best use, to impose a levy on income from rural properties, and to place an inheritance tax on rural properties within the jurisdiction were defeated.

On November 21, 1961, a Constitutional amendment of great significance to the municipalities was passed. Though its most important feature was to open up major new inputs of money by the federal government to the municipalities, it also widened municipal demand capabilities by transferring two taxes, previously collected by the states, to local government. The first of these was the rural property tax, thus giving the municipalities complete control over this source of revenue. The second was the real-estate transfer tax. These new sources, though overshadowed by the tax-sharing provisions of the amendment, were of no little significance. In 1963 they accounted for about 12 per cent of municipal revenue. The effect of the 1961 amendment, Ferreira has commented, was to cause another major change in the structure of government in Brazil. As 1891 had represented a shift from central to state dominance, the 1961 amendment declared the "definitive" abandonment of "statism in favor of municipalism."[16]

Resource Inputs to the System—to 1964

DEVELOPMENT OF TAX-SHARING POLICIES

The rather severe constraints which were placed on the national municipal system were not compatible with a growing insistence that

---

[16] Ibid.

local communities have greater freedom to govern themselves. Rather than relax these constraints appreciably, the Brazilian pattern has been to expand the inputs from higher levels of government to the resource-pressed municipalities. In providing such inputs, a government may follow one of two general approaches. It may grant monies to other jurisdictions on the basis of such conditions as it desires to impose. These are essentially gifts which one level of government gives to help another. The United States government has relied heavily on such grants, which tend to impose rather stringent conditions on the recipients. The second approach is tax sharing, in which one unit of government simply performs the administrative chores for another. In the United States, for example, we typically pay one state gasoline tax; but this tax is distributed, by right, among several jurisdictions. While the two approaches blend into each other, there are certainly psychological differences. In the latter case, the jurisdiction is receiving its own money, rather than a gift.

The Brazilian pattern has tended to be one of tax sharing. It began with the Constitution of 1934, at which time it was specified that the business and industry tax be levied at the state level and be shared 50-50 with the municipalities. The business and industry tax then moved from a sharing basis to complete local control in 1946. The 1934 document also provided that 20 per cent of any new taxes imposed by the state or national governments should be shared with the municipalities. While the real purpose of this latter provision was to make it uninteresting to impose new taxes at the state or national level and thus to maintain the established tax pattern, the provision undoubtedly also had the effect of further legitimating the tax-sharing idea. The Vargas Constitution of 1937 eliminated this condition, leaving the central government free to impose such new taxes as it desired.

Tax sharing took a major step forward in 1940 when a single tax on oil and other combustible products was passed. The income from this levy was earmarked for road and highway work and was to be shared by the national, state, and local governments. The formula worked out at that time for the distribution of these funds has tended to persist. The national municipal system has received 12 per cent of the total and the states 48 per cent; but in fact, the tax has not been a major source of income.

1946 CONSTITUTION AND NEW INPUTS

The Constitution of 1946 gave sharp, new impetus to the idea of tax sharing, particularly in the introduction of two provisions. The first of these (Article VI, Par. 4) directed the federal government to share 10 per cent of its income-tax revenues with the national municipal system, with the exception of the capital cities of the states. One string was attached—that at least half of the receipts should be spent on rural development. The states were also ordered to share their revenues with the municipalities. Article 20 required that when the state taxes collected in a municipality exceeded the total income "of any nature" of the community municipal system, 30 per cent of the overage had to be sent back to the municipality. Only one state tax, on the export of goods, was exempted from this calculation. Capital cities were not included.[17]

The Constitution also maintained the sharing aspects of the single tax on combustibles, with the requirement that 60 per cent of the proceeds would go to state and local levels of government, to be distributed on the basis of population, land area, and the consumption and production of the products taxed. In addition, the Constitution reinstituted the requirement that 20 per cent of any new taxes levied by the national or state governments should be shared with the municipalities.

The 1961 amendment to the Constitution, which gave the municipalities greater freedom to make demands, was even more significant for its enlargement of the obligation of the federal government to make inputs to the national municipal system. First, the share of the income tax to be directed to the municipalities was raised from 10 per cent to 15 per cent; second, the municipalities were to receive 10 per cent of the excise tax, by all odds the most productive of the federal revenue sources. To provide some indication of the potential meaning of this change, it may be noted that the national municipal system collected only about 24 billion cruzeiros in taxes and service fees in 1960. In that same year, the national government received about 83 billion cruzeiros

---

[17] For a complete picture of this tax and its rationale, see Carlos Alberto A. de Carvalho Pinto, "O Artigo 20 da Constitutição Federal e as Capitais," *Revista de Administração Municipal,* 72:328–343. (September–October 1965).

in excise taxes and 62 billion cruzeiros in income taxes. Thus, the total amount to be shared with the municipalities was 17.6 billion cruzeiros, a whopping 70 per cent of the total tax income of the national municipal system. The scale of this tax-sharing program is also evidenced by the proportion of national revenue, 8 per cent, that was to be diverted to the municipalities, essentially without strings attached.

The basis of the sharing retained the simple prescriptions of the 1946 Constitution. Each municipality was to share equally in the inputs, including the state capitals which had been excluded by the 1946 Constitution. While the stipulation that 50 per cent of the funds be spent for rural development remained in the provision for income-tax sharing, there was no such requirement with regard to funds from the excise tax.

COLLECTING THE MONEY

The rain of gold never reached the torrential proportions indicated by the Constitutional amendment. The central government simply never met its obligations to provide the indicated inputs; and the great majority of states similarly failed to fulfill the requirement of Article 20 that they return 30 per cent of their excess collections to the local level.

Transfers from the income and excise taxes were the most crucial to the national municipal system. According to the initial procedures adopted to implement the 1946 Constitution, municipalities were to receive funds on a monthly basis. However, that never occurred. In 1949 and 1950, collections for the preceding year were shared in September, with the payment stepped up to July in 1951. In view of the apparent impossibility of meeting the monthly schedule of payments, the Congress passed a law in 1951 providing that the municipal shares should be distributed by September 1 of each year. From 1952 to 1954, the law was observed.

Then, as Brazil began its period of accelerated industrial progress under Juscelino Kubitschek, the payments became slower. Not infrequently, they were not even made in the year they were due. The situation continued to worsen to the time of passage of the Constitutional amendment in 1961. In that amendment, there was a provision that payments be made on a Constitutionally-prescribed schedule, a lump sum to be paid by September 30 in the case of the income tax and single payment to be made by December 31 in the case of the excise tax.

Even a Constitutional amendment, however, did not improve the situation as Brazil passed through a period of extreme national turbulence. In 1962 income-tax transfers were made in the last quarter of the year, and excise shares were not distributed. In 1963 the cities did get one-quarter of the amount due on the excise account; but no more had been paid to 1965. In December 1963 the income-tax share was provided; again, nothing came from the excise source. In the year of the revolution (1964) nothing at all was transferred from either source. Since that time, payments have been made but not in the amounts provided in the Constitution.

In analyzing the record of these collection problems, it seems useful to relate, once again, these inputs to the two types of outputs described, those that are political and those that are of a service nature. While it may be difficult to argue that the system of transfer payments arose specifically to finance political outputs, it does appear that the pattern adopted tended to have little relevance to service outputs. The insistence on equal payments to all municipalities has had the effect of making federal funds mighty important to the smaller units with the least service obligations. On the other hand, the great cities like São Paulo, Recife, and Belo Horizonte have found the amount of very little significance. Thus, the members of the national municipal system who might be expected to make the most insistent demands and for whom the delay in payments would have the most serious social and political repercussions have not had a reason to interest themselves in the problem. They typically have sought individual and direct support from the national government.

A second factor that has tended to minimize the linkage of inputs to service outputs has been the lack of specific program objectives to which the monies transferred are tied. Except for the Constitutional requirement that half the income-tax monies be spent on rural development, there have been no strings attached. There have been no formal, stated expectations of service outputs to be produced in return for the inputs provided. Nor has there been any real belief that the half of the municipalities which have received the bulk of their funds from this source would be either motivated toward, or capable of, producing service outputs. As de Mello has written, ". . . these municipalities do not have the administrative structure, nor the organized services and programs, to apply resources of this scale rationally."[18]

It is possible, then, that the national government, pressed for resource inputs on many fronts, curtailed its transfers of money to the municipalities because there was little expectation of service output. A sharply reduced level of sharing was sufficient to meet political necessities, as is evidenced by the fact that over half of the municipalities still received 70–80 per cent of their revenues from this source. Also, within the national municipal system, the reduced level of transfers still accounted for about 22 per cent of total income in 1962. Finally, the necessity to meet increasing service demands in the large urban areas could not in any case be met by the tax-sharing plan in effect. If the federal government had fully met its commitment, the outlay of perhaps 8 per cent of the total income of the national government would have little effect on metropolitan services.

The experience with state sharing of revenue has shown an even more flagrant disregard of Constitutional prescription. Mayor Ferreira reports that, after 19 years of experience, 18 of the states and all of the territories had failed to make any payment at all to their municipalities.[19] De Mello has commented that only three states, all in the south (Rio Grande do Sul, São Paulo, and Santa Catarina), met this obligation regularly. "Some others," he says, "have made sporadic efforts in this direction, generally for political reasons, but the majority, with Minas Gerais in the lead, have simply not been disposed to meet this Constitutional provision."[20]

The 1959 survey of the Brazilian Institute of Municipal Administration revealed the same geographic characteristic noted by de Mello. Unfortunately, the Institute's questionnaire was not able to distinguish between those municipalities which had the right to a sharing because of excess collections and those which did not. Even so, approximately 83 per cent of the municipalities in the south (647 of 783) reported receipt of such funds. This situation was in sharp contrast to that in other parts of the country, where the percentage of nonrecipients ranged from 82 per cent to 96 per cent.[21]

---

[18] De Mello, *Problemas Institucionais,* p. 21.

[19] Ferreira, p. 423.

[20] De Mello, *Problemas Institucionais,* p. 23.

[21] *Municípios do Brasil* (Rio de Janeiro: Instituto Brasileiro de Administração Municipal, 1960), p. 62–63.

Again, the possibility of a relationship between the willingness to provide inputs and expectations of service outputs may be noted. Two of the three states in which payments were regularized are regarded as having the highest level of local government service in the country, São Paulo and Rio Grande do Sul. Given its relatively low level of urbanization and industrialization, Santa Catarina also spent a proportionately high amount on local government services. In effect, then, the data seem to bear out the prediction that inputs from higher levels of government would tend to be greatest where service outputs are highest.

In contrast to the general failure of the federal and state governments to share revenues, the experience with the oil and combustibles single tax seems to have been quite different. Here, it will be remembered, states get 48 per cent of revenue collected and the municipalities get 12 per cent. Criteria have been established for the sharing, based essentially on need and contribution; and the proceeds of the tax are earmarked for road purposes. A similar single tax now applies to consumption of electrical energy, from which the national municipal system receives a 10 per cent share. Noting that the expenditure of these resources is subject to the control of "competent federal authorities," de Mello regards the system as "very satisfactory," with few charges of misuse of funds.[22] Data presented in the 1959 survey certainly support this contention; over 90 per cent of the municipalities declared they had received their share of monies from this source. Furthermore, payments tended to be more current than was the case in the other transfers.[23] Again it should be noted that the single-tax-sharing pattern provided a more distinct goal, called for closer supervision, and was more specific in relating the level of inputs to output requirements. In short, money may have been forthcoming because there was a fair anticipation of the production of service outputs.

Inputs and Their Effect on Demands

The experience in Brazil has revealed the inherent dilemma faced in striking a rough balance between locally produced supports and centrally endowed supports. The local municipal government is con-

[22] De Mello, *Problemas Institucionais,* pp. 20–21.
[23] *Municípios do Brasil,* p. 63.

strained by political, economic, and administrative considerations with regard to the demands it can make on its community environment. Even in the best of circumstances, for example, it would not be wise to levy an export tax at the municipal level. On the other hand, there are many compelling reasons—of a political, economic, and administrative nature—why the community should support much of its local government activity.

The effect of too many resource inputs from higher levels of government is to reduce the incentive to make demands on the community for supports. Conversely, a failure to provide inputs from above, and thus implicitly to assume that demands will be made by the community municipal system on its environment, is to invite very substantial discrepancy in levels of performance and service. The rich will typically do well; the poor badly.

To a considerable degree, Brazil has seemed, under its 1946–1966 tax pattern, to secure the worst of both worlds. The 1961 expenditure levels of São Paulo (with an Urbanization Index of 48) were about three times those of Pernambuco (with an Index of 30). Presumably, the difference in levels of service performances was at least as great. It should be remembered, too, that the big cities have received very little of the federal money, even though they have housed major portions of the population. In effect, the great municipalities have had to make disproportionately heavy support demands on their communities.

On the other hand, Brazil demonstrates that too great an infusion of resources from higher levels can reduce the incentive to make demands. In Santa Catarina and Rio Grande do Sul, where the states have been faithful in meeting their obligations, it is common for more than 50 per cent of a municipality's income to be derived from transfer payments. The 1965 budget of Joinville, in Santa Catarina, for example, anticipated 45 per cent of the municipality's revenue from the sharing of excess state collection. Inevitably, these municipalities have scaled down their demands on the local community. De Mello has noted that in Rio Grande do Sul and Santa Catarina ". . . the level of productivity of the municipal tax system is strangely low, as compared with other less prosperous states."[24] He then underscores a problem that has frequently occurred in the administration of subventions where taxes

---

[24] De Mello, *Problemas Institucionais,* p. 23.

collected are regarded as a criterion of the willingness of the community to tax itself. Where the state must share all money obtained above the level of local tax collections, there is an incentive to reduce demands on the community. The lower the local tax take, the greater the participation in state revenues.

Data developed in the 1959 nationwide survey add further support to the hypothesis that the greater the amount of inputs from higher levels of government, the less the inclination to make demands on the community. In the survey, municipalities were grouped in four population classes. Generally speaking, the smaller the municipality the greater its dependence on shared revenues. Responses to the various questions were then analyzed in terms of these groups. Among the questions were several dealing with tax administration, of which three seem particularly relevant for this discussion. They asked whether the municipality had a tax code, whether it had an up-to-date tax map, and whether the business and industry tax was levied according to a flat schedule or according to some index of gross receipts. An inspection of the data reveals quite clearly that the smaller the municipality, the less apt it was to have a tax code, to have an up-to-date tax map, and to use gross receipts as basis for the business and industry levy.[25]

Thus there are many questions that can be raised about the appropriate mix of inputs to the national municipal system. Essentially, the problem is one of finding the golden mean between a maximum of local support and provision for supports from higher levels of government to enable the national municipal system to meet its goals. Brazil has given a great deal of attention to the separation of tax sources among its three levels of government, with the result that the municipalities have been quite limited in the amount and types of demands they can make. These restrictions, which reduce the capability of the local unit to finance itself, inevitably call into question the nature and extent of supports to be provided by higher levels of government. In general such supports have been most important to the small communities and have probably reduced the incentive to make demands on the local environment. The great metropolitan cities, in which such a large percentage of Brazil's population lives, have been virtually unaffected. How, then, to establish the balance?

---

[25] *Municípios do Brasil,* pp. 54–61.

Revolution, Reform—Centralization?

Even before the 1964 revolution, the kinds of problems noted above were being recognized in Brazil. In late 1962 the Reform Commission of the Ministry of Finance was established under the leadership of Dr. Luis Simões Lopes, President of the Getulio Vargas Foundation. Its obligations concerned particularly the reform of tax policy and administration in Brazil. With the revolution, the work of the Commission took on new importance, at least partly because it was clear that the decisions of the new government would revolve around criteria of economic efficiency.

The Shoup report was an early product of the Commission's work. Carl F. Shoup, an eminent economist from Columbia University, visited Brazil for one month in August 1964 and made a number of recommendations on tax policy, contained in his *The Tax System of Brazil*. Among his proposals were these: (a) repeal of the municipal sharing of national income and excise tax funds; (b) repeal of the municipal sharing of state excess tax collections; (c) introduction of formula-type grants-in-aid on the United States model; (d) transfer of the rural land tax from the municipalities to the state or federal level; (e) a maximum rate of 1 per cent on real-estate transfer taxes; and (f) improvement in assessment administration of the municipal real-estate taxes. In addition, Professor Shoup proposed that the basic source of revenue for the states, the cascade-type sales tax, be replaced by a single-stage levy.[26]

Shortly after Professor Shoup finished his report, Congress passed Constitutional Amendment 10, in November 1964, which transferred the administration of the rural property tax to the national level. In keeping with the recommendations of the Columbia professor, the real intent of this change was to enable the national government to use the tax as a weapon to achieve rural land redistribution and reform. The amendment specified that the proceeds of the tax would be returned, 100 per cent, to the municipalities in which the land was located. Apparently to compensate for the loss of local control of the rural land tax, the Congress also passed a law at about the same time assigning 20

---

[26] Shoup, pp. 17–24.

per cent of the tax on minerals to the national municipal system. Thus, as of the end of 1964, the municipalities had lost control of a tax but not its revenue; and the national municipal system had been accorded a substantial share of another federal tax.

For more than a year after the revolution, the Reform Commission was debating a wholesale revision of the nation's tax policy. The proposed Constitutional amendment that emerged in 1965 represented a sharp break with the past. It was, as de Mello wrote, an essentially economic document, ". . . characterized by its effort to give an economic orientation to the different taxes and to the tax system as a whole. Thus, it seeks to avoid the superimposition of taxes of the same nature, reducing the numbers of taxes, with elimination of various imposts and the specification in precise form of the field of applicability of various others."[27] To indicate the "purely economic inspiration" of the document, de Mello noted that the report was organized in terms of the economic classification of taxes, rather than according to the units of government which would be involved.

In de Mello's judgment, the proposed amendment was "totally disastrous" for the national municipal system. He estimated that the system would lose about 60 per cent of its income. The municipalities would be ". . . annulled, practically speaking, as units of government, not only destroying their financial autonomy but also destroying their political-administrative autonomy."[28] Such strong words, timed to influence the course of decision in a municipal matter, had never before come from the eminent director of the Brazilian Institute of Municipal Administration (IBAM). Indeed, the organization had prided its technical-neutral reputation and its separation from the special-interest pleadings of the "municipalists." However, the proposals were so detrimental to the institutional status of the municipalities, that is, to their autonomy, that de Mello's organization chose to depart from its own tradition and to speak out.

The proposed amendment followed rather generally the recommendations of the Shoup report, in that the cascade-type sales tax was marked for elimination. On the other hand, the suggestion that some tax overlapping be permitted was sacrificed in favor of the separation

---

[27] De Mello, "A Discriminação," p. 3.
[28] Ibid., p. 7.

of sources and of the practice of tax sharing to get revenues from one level to another. Perhaps the most significant evidence of this increased commitment to sharing was the introduction of state participation in federal revenues. With regard to the national municipal system, however, the Reform Commission proposed a major cut. This proposal involved a generally scaled-down level of sharing of the various federal resources and set new constraints on the ability of the individual municipality to impose demands on its environment. The business and industry tax, which had yielded 42 per cent of the locally collected revenue to the national municipal system in 1962, was to be prohibited; the real-estate transfer tax, accounting for over 11 per cent of total revenue, was to be returned to the states; and licenses, stamp taxes, and levies on games and amusements, representing over 8 per cent of local income, were also proscribed.

The proposal reduced the municipal share in the excise tax from 10 to 8 per cent, in the income tax from 15 to 8 per cent; and the states and municipalities were to have their 60 per cent share in the single taxes on combustibles and electric energy reduced to 50 per cent. The mandate that the states share the overage of their collections with the municipalities was eliminated, but with the compensation that 15 per cent of the revenue from the new single-stage sales tax be shared with the municipality in whose jurisdiction it was collected.

Hence a major point of concern was the gross amount of funds to be made available to the national municipal system. Though he admitted that the tax sharing of the past had stimulated an unwarranted expansion in the number of municipalities and perhaps some waste in the use of funds, de Mello argued that the answer rested elsewhere than in the reduction of resources to the municipalities. He declared that the institutionalization of the municipalities had come primarily from increasing the amounts of inputs provided. The growth in resources, he pointed out, had been continuous since 1934, in accord with ". . . an expansion of understanding of the importance of the nation's interior to our economic and social development and the deep roots of our political development."[29]

It is interesting, however, that the scale of inputs was only one cause of alarm. The other preoccupation, quite understandably, was

[29] Ibid., p. 12.

with the discretion accorded the national government in the distribution of tax shares. The proposed amendment left the details of the sharing to implementing statutes and to administrative rules.

De Mello saw the new discretion granted the central government as a major blow to local autonomy. While he did not object to specifying the purposes for which the monies might be used, he was most insistent that the pattern of equal shares was right for a country in Brazil's stage of development. The vitality and autonomy of the individual municipality, he said, depended on its right to receive its share of funds, without being subject to the whims of higher levels of government; and this autonomy was particularly necessary for the balanced development of the country. He put the point in the following terms:

Presently, even more than in 1946, it is difficult to attack the system which strengthened municipal revenues through tax shares, which are equally important to each municipality. If we accept the premise that the financial vitality of the small municipalities of the interior cannot be obtained entirely through their own revenue sources, given the technical limitations and the implied fiscal policy, such a system ought to be complemented by the participation of the municipality in federal and state revenues. Further, if we take into account the enormous economic inequalities of the various regions and subregions of the country, we must accept tax sharing along the lines instituted by the 1946 Constitution, as a measure perfectly consonant with our federal regime.[30]

. . . The truth is . . . the present criterion for shared revenues contains a substantial portion of political sophistication, for it promotes national solidarity by redistributing to the poor municipalities and regions part of the resources collected by the Union in the more economically favored areas.[31]

Constitutional Amendment 18, made official on December 6, 1965, included some concessions to the de Mello line of argument but essentially followed the master lines of the original proposal. It took effect on January 1, 1967, and its provisions were not changed appreciably by the new Constitution approved by the Brazilian Congress in January 1967.

One of the major concessions was the acceptance of Shoup's idea of overlapping tax powers. The new amendment provided that not only

[30] De Mello, *Problemas Institucionais,* p. 20.
[31] De Mello, "A Discriminação," p. 12–13.

the state but also the municipality might levy a sales tax not to exceed 20 per cent of that imposed by the state. Designed to take the place of the previously lucrative business and industry tax, the overlap was called by Professor Carlos V. de A. Amaral the "great innovation" in the new tax system.[32] Over-all, however, increased constraints were placed on the municipality's power to make demands on its environment. Lost were the real-estate transfer tax, license taxes, stamp taxes, and levies on amusements, as well as the business and industry impost. Amaral believed that there would be new pressure to improve the productivity of the property tax; but here the difficulty was to provide the municipality with the administrative mechanism capable of carrying out such a task. The removal of a number of taxes and the substitution of a source with specific limitations must be regarded as a net loss to the municipality's demand capability. Its over-all revenue potential was reduced; and it also was less free to choose among possible targets for its demands. On the other hand, the acceptance of the tax-overlap principle may have been an important gain for the future institutional development of the national municipal system.

Undoubtedly the most significant feature of the Constitutional amendment was the elimination of the "equal shares" formula for distribution of excise and income taxes. While the Constitutional strings remained loose, with only the prescription that 50 per cent of such monies had to go for capital outlays, the clear implication was that the national government would set new standards and criteria for the sharing program. Thus the question in early 1967 was whether Brazil's development had reached ". . . a stage of objectivity and political isolation which permits the functioning of a system of aids and subventions free from political-party injunctions and the other inevitable conditions which can result in total control of the municipalities by the federal government."[33]

While the attaching of strings was by far the most important element in the amendment, also significant was the provision that reduced the total amount of inputs from higher levels to the municipalities. The reduction of inputs was not, however, as great as had originally been proposed. The sharing of excess state revenues was

---

[32] Carlos V. de A. Amaral, "O Municipio na Nova Discriminação de Rendas," *Revista de Administração Municipal,* 76:202 (May–June 1966).

[33] De Mello, "A Discriminação," p. 14.

eliminated, which really affected only three states. The biggest reduction for the national municipal system was in the income share, which dropped from 15 to 10 per cent. The other national revenues, however, maintained previous distribution percentages. Municipalities in individual states received extra jolts from the reform, as special types of taxes were eliminated. In the state of Rio Grande do Sul, for example, the municipalities shared 40 per cent in a "transport charge"; and in the state of São Paulo the municipalities also received 40 per cent of a state tax on transactions.

Thus the new amendment's tax-sharing provisions had their effect on the institutional status of the municipalities. Regardless of how the central government may operate, the elimination of the equal-shares formula represented a net reduction in the autonomy of the municipalities by denying them the federal funds as a matter of right. In addition, the municipalities ended up with a smaller total pie.

What the effect of these changes will be on the great metropolitan municipalities, which were outside the tax-sharing pattern of the old system, is not entirely clear. While they will now be eligible to participate in the various shared revenues, their capability to produce their own supports has been greatly restricted. In 1963, for example, the capital cities of the country got 56 per cent of their tax revenues from the business and industry levy; and the taxes abolished amounted to 72 per cent of the total collected. Whether the new sales tax and the shares of federal revenues will be sufficient to make up the difference appears to be doubtful. Furthermore, the big cities' fiscal fortunes will depend on the federal government's willingness and ability to pay its obligations. The experience of the past does not provide much encouragement for the future.

Summary

It is certainly no great revelation that resource inputs are required by any system. Nor is it particularly new that autonomy, and therefore institutionalization, is dependent upon resource inputs that are (a) large enough in scale to produce valued outputs and (b) sufficiently free of strings to allow the institution to set its own goals and objectives.

I have suggested that there is a national municipal system in Brazil, which, while it does not contain the normal system properties, exists because relevant parts of the environment choose to think it exists. In many respects this national municipal system has been achieving an increasing degree of institutionalization since the founding of the republic in 1891; and the pace quickened with the Constitution of 1934. With the "municipalist" Constitution of 1946, which formally recognized three levels of government in Brazil, a high degree of "official" institutionalization had been reached.

However, no system can produce valued outputs without importing energy. The municipalities in Brazil have traditionally been the poor cousins; and even their new status of 1946 did not automatically endow them with the flow of resources that would have enabled them to move beyond their traditional concern with political outputs toward the broad spectrum of service outputs. Resources should not be taken here to mean solely money, but should also reflect the human and organizational capabilities that money over a longer period makes possible. As we saw in the preceding chapter, the processing capabilities of the community municipal systems have been very low. These problems, as well as rigid Constitutional constraints on the demands that can be made, has limited appreciably the extent to which the individual municipality has been able to secure inputs from its own environment.

At the level of the national municipal system, the struggle to secure an adequate flow of inputs to obtain autonomy, stability, and therefore institutionalization, reached a high point in 1961. Yet, generous as the formal arrangements were, the money never came through in the amounts prescribed. It might be argued that this result was to be predicted. Resources have been sufficient to meet political-output needs in the great majority of municipalities; what has not been done is to provide supports for service outputs.

The policy of tax sharing on a basis of equality and without strings attached has had other problems. It has made the relationship between input and output unclear. Nobody, for example, has any firm idea how the billions of income-tax shares have contributed to the work of the municipality. Further, the equal-shares system has left the big cities virtually outside the network, has sparked the creation of economically questionable municipalities, and has reduced the incentive in many of the municipalities to make desired demands for support on their communities.

The tax structure that took effect on January 1, 1967, appears to be a backward step in the process of institutionalizing the national municipal system. It has placed increased limits on the capability of the municipality to make demands on its environment. It appears to reduce the over-all levels of support to the national municipal system. And, most important, it places very substantial portions of municipal resources at the discretion of the central government. On the other hand, the traditional barrier against tax overlapping has now been breached. The municipalities, as well as the states, may levy a sales tax. Furthermore, a wise and mature central government could use the considerable amounts of tax shares to launch new programs that would enable the municipalities to achieve status as producers of valued outputs in the community environment. It seems obvious that these tax-share policies and their administration will go a long way toward defining the role of the municipalities in Brazil's political system in the years ahead.

CHAPTER EIGHT

THE MUNICIPALITY IN THE GOVERNANCE OF A METROPOLIS: A CASE STUDY

When the city of Rio de Janeiro became Brazil's twenty-first state (Guanabara) in 1960, it faced serious problems. A densely populated community of more than 3,000,000 people, its territory was actually less than that of many municipalities. A basic question was how to organize itself. Should it follow the pattern of the rest of the states and create municipalities?

This case study approaches the municipal problem of Brazil in a somewhat different context. It will examine the way in which the role of the municipality in the organization of a great metropolitan community was addressed and debated.

For comparative purposes it is also interesting to observe that this case involves a problem which is directly the reverse of that which we have experienced in the United States. In the United States, the thrust of virtually all metropolitan-reform movements has been toward the expansion of the powers of an existing level of government or the creation of a larger new one. The opposite was true in Guanabara. The integration of the governmental structure was complete. The state government had a very broad area of responsibility and authority. The status quo was thus represented by organizational integration, and fragmentation was the objective of the proposed organizational change.

Background: Rio

While São Paulo's great manufacturing enterprises make it the Chicago of Brazil, Rio de Janeiro retains first place in the affections of

Brazilians. Rio is indeed a beautiful and cosmopolitan city, with its bays and mountains providing opportunities for endless surprise and interest. The metropolitan area has a total of about 5,000,000 people, approximately 70 per cent of whom reside in the state of Guanabara. The direction of urban growth outside the state has generally been in two directions: north along the Rio-São Paulo highway and east across Guanabara Bay to Niterói. While there are, consequently, some problems of metropolitan jurisdiction, the shape of the land and the fact that a large share of the population resides within the state of Guanabara tend to lessen these complications considerably.

In 1965 the city of Rio celebrated its four hundredth anniversary. For almost half that time it served as the capital of Brazil. When the Portuguese colony of Brazil was raised to the category of vice-kingdom in 1763, the capital was moved from Salvador to Rio. The city continued in that status until 1960, when President Juscelino Kubitschek officially moved the seat of government to the interior capital of Brasília.

Rio's position as the government center inevitably had a great influence on its political development; for its special status left relatively little opportunity for the evolution of any grass-roots institutions. In 1834 an amendment to the Constitution gave Rio legal recognition as a neutral municipality, a Federal District; and this action removed it from its jurisdictional relationship with the province of Rio de Janeiro. Thus today the city of Rio de Janeiro is not located in the state of Rio de Janeiro, in which, incidentally, the metropolitan spillover is occurring. Under the Crown, the Federal District had no autonomy. With the establishment of a republic, however, an organic law for the government of the District evolved. This law made the mayor the appointee of the President of Brazil, but also provided for an elective legislative body. This broad pattern of government continued until the transfer of the capital.

Two basic consequences for the electorate appear to have emerged from Rio's lengthy experience as the federal capital: (a) there was no background in, and little understanding of, the need for a multiplicity of jurisdictions to administer metropolitan services; and (b) there was little faith in the effective operation of democratic institutions at the local level. Rio was seen as existing—rather badly—on the sufferance of the national government; and the District legislature was regarded as the supreme example of political venality. So poor were the urban services, and so low the confidence in self-government, that real questions were raised whether the city could ever survive as a truly independent entity.

The change of the capital to Brasília on April 21, 1960, did not in itself raise any serious question as to the future of the old Federal District. Since the Constitution of 1891, policies calling for a move of the capital to the interior had been voiced, with the further proviso that Rio was to be given statehood. The 1946 Constitution specified that Rio would become the state of Guanabara; and Brazil's twenty-first state was born on the day that the new Federal District came into being. It also assumed the title of "smallest state in the Union."

Thus 1960 was a highly significant period in the history of the "marvelous city." In April it became a state; in October it elected its first governor and its first state legislature; and in December these new officers assumed their seats.

Origins of the Problem

The Constitution for the new state of Guanabara was not fashioned by a constituent body solely established for that purpose. Instead, the state legislature was assigned the dual function of shaping a new charter and at the same time making more immediate policies within the framework of the then existing district organic law.

This relatively unusual circumstance has significance for the present analysis. The lawgivers of the new state had a problem of relating the traditions of Rio to the Constitutional norms of the nation. These norms called for the creation of municipalities. The tradition of the old Federal District, however, was in conflict with such a standard. Furthermore, a problem of such perplexing proportions had to be faced by a part-time constituent assembly—one, incidentally, which was also under great time pressures to finish the basic policy lines for a state that was already in being and functioning. The consequence was that Constitutional debates were relatively brief and were sandwiched in among pressing immediate issues, and the involvement of any outside interests was limited.

These debates were included in the regular daily record of the state assembly; and, while the question of the municipalities was certainly not ignored, a general impression is that the matter was not discussed exhaustively.[1]

Operating under these imperatives, the assembly of the state of Guanabara actually completed its work rather quickly; and the Constitution was officially enacted on March 27, 1961. While the resulting document was generally given high praise, it did contain an unusual provision for the handling of the municipal question. The Constitution called for the staging of a plebiscite on April 21, 1963, to allow the citizens to decide whether they wanted municipalities or not.

Three other provisions of the Constitution also were relevant to the establishment of municipalities. The first set standards for any municipalities that might be created, declaring that they should be "conditioned to the peculiarities of the region, to the geo-economic, demographic and financial conditions, and to the possibilities of maintaining municipal public services" (Title IV, art. 52). Second, the Constitution indicated that the plebiscite should answer only the broad question of whether municipalities should be created or not; one month after the plebiscite the state assembly was to take the "necessary measures for the complete fulfillment of the popular deliberation" (Article 9 of the Transitory Provisions). Finally, in Article 8 of the Transitory Provisions, the Constitution required that an eight-man commission, with equal representation from the legislative and executive branches, be established within 90 days. The commission was to "realize studies" on the matter.

As Aldney Peixoto has written, "Only the short time which the Constituent Assembly had available and the importance of the problem could justify the failure to resolve it immediately."[2]

---

[1] The writer carefully reviewed the entire record of the assembly, a task made more difficult by the lack of an index. It was anticipated that the review of these debates would become an important part of the present study, and pages were noted for later photocopying. However, all these materials, including the documents themselves, were in a car which was stolen in November 1963. The car was returned 10 days later, but the papers had been thrown away. The event was particularly sad because there are few complete copies of assembly debates; the library of the Getulio Vargas Foundation has not been able to replace them completely.

[2] Aldney Peixoto, "Estrutura Geográfica do Estado da Guanabara," in Comissão Especial sôbre a Organização Municipal do Estado, *Subsídios para o Plebiscito sobre a Divisão do Estado em Municípios* (Rio de Janeiro: Assembléia Legislativa do Estado da Guanabara, 1963), p. 135.

The complexities in the situation were certainly significant. Though the federal Constitution did not specifically require the creation of municipalities, many people thought that such an imperative was implicitly stated. Furthermore, the municipal question had important financing implications. Certain taxes, particularly those on land and property, were assigned by the federal Constitution to the municipalities, and it was estimated that these imposts represented about one-fourth of the income of the state. Certain federal subsidies were also granted solely to the municipal levels.

Because of these problems, three different kinds of alternatives were presented at the time of the Constitutional discussions. First, there were suggestions for the creation of a municipal system within the state solely for its own worth. The second proposal was to create a single municipality, coterminous with the boundaries of the state, which would levy taxes of exclusive municipal competence and would receive federal funds. Third, the idea was proposed to resolve the problem by once again making the city of Rio de Janeiro a part of the state of Rio de Janeiro. In the debates, it appeared that members of the Labor Party tended most often to defend the creation of municipalities, and those of the conservative National Democratic Union tended to be in opposition. The single municipality was obviously an expedient; and the fusion with the state of Rio de Janeiro probably no more than romanticism.

In this environment, it was Professor Themistocles Cavalcanti, one of Brazil's most eminent scholars of administrative law and government, who took the leadership in espousing the plebiscite. He later pointed out that the "first difficulty" was the identification of a basis upon which to divide the state. He said that the old Federal District was a "true chaos" in terms of its decentralization patterns, with virtually every function distributed among a different number of districts. "Any undertaking would therefore be extremely difficult," he claimed.[3] Commenting on the origins of the plebiscite, the leftist daily newspaper *Última Hora* later noted, "The question of whether to transform Guanabara into municipalities began with the installation of the

---

[3] Themistocles Brandão Cavalcanti, "Divisão do Estado da Guanabara em Municípios," in Comissão Especial sôbre a Organização Municipal do Estado, *O Problema da Divisão do Estado da Guanabara em Municípios* (Rio de Janeiro: Assembléia Legislativa do Estado da Guanabara, 1962), p. 10.

Constituent Assembly. In a few weeks, the problem became a matter of common concern in the press, radio, and television. It was then that constituent-deputy Themistocles Cavalcanti suggested the realization of the plebiscite in order to avoid precipitate solutions."[4]

As events unfolded, the delay was favorable to the opponents of municipalization. In June 1961, only a few months after the promulgation of the Guanabara Constitution, the federal Congress approved Amendment 3. Its Article 5 said, "To the states, which are constituted without municipalities after September 19, 1946, in view of local peculiarities, are assigned also the taxes foreseen in Article 29." Thus Amendment 3 made it possible for the State of Guanabara to collect municipal taxes. Barbosa Lima Sobrinho wrote that the "problem was resolved." He said that the idea of the plebiscite had only been an "expedient" because the legislators feared to lose the municipal taxes. They had been "at the point" of accepting the division of the state in order to avoid the loss of these funds.[5]

The Special Commission on the Municipal Organization of the State was formed with a "blue ribbon" membership. The chairman was Professor Aliomar Baleeiro, an outstanding authority on public finance and a long-time member of the national Congress; Professor Cavalcanti; Saldanha Coelho, the leader of the Labor Party in the state assembly; Prado Kelly, an outstanding lawyer; and Eurico Sequeira, a bureaucrat of reputation. The Commission printed two reports, one in 1962 and one in 1963. Its recommendation against municipal division was written by Prado Kelly and, though not published, was well publicized in the newspapers.

The Alternative Proposals

It seemed quite apparent that the execution of the Constitutional mandate would involve considerable frustration for the voting public. The electorate was to opine on its desire for a municipal level of government, but the question was abstract in the extreme. How many municipalities? Doing what things? With what kinds of costs? There

---

[4] *Última Hora,* April 8, 1963.

[5] Barbosa Lima Sobrinho, "Fartura de Plebiscitos," *Jornal do Brasil,* April 21, 1963.

was even a question as to whether the use of the word "division" was proper. Some thought the real issue involved "creation" of municipalities. In any case, the parameters of the problem posed to the electorate were very different from those known in the United States. Typically, the United States citizen has been faced with a detailed proposal about which he has very little knowledge. But the specifics are available. In Guanabara, anyone was free to choose his own boundaries in approaching the general question of municipalization.

In the course of the election campaign, at least eight different approaches to municipal organization were proposed. Of these, the opposing forces would appear to have proposed four, and the promunicipal segment the other four.

In seeking to prevent the development of a municipal level of government, the opponents tended to concentrate on three different approaches to metropolitan change. The first of these involved the merger of the states of Guanabara and Rio de Janeiro. The argument was that lesser solutions did not meet the problem and that Guanabara's natural social and political integrity was being destroyed in the process. Governor Carlos Lacerda, whose party was the conservative National Democratic Union, joined in this argument. It seemed generally agreed, though, that such a merger would never take place. A second approach was the one-city idea. However, this idea was obviously a tax instrumentality, and its need had been obviated by the amendment to the federal Constitution.

The third approach taken by the pro-state people involved proposals that fairly clearly put the concept of municipal division in its worst light. The Special Commission based its studies on the creation of four municipalities in the state; and the president of the state assembly, who wrote a principal paper for the Special Commission, suggested the alternative of 21 municipalities, in accord with the 21 regional administrations being developed by Governor Lacerda.

The choice of the four-municipality concept by the Special Commission was not explained; but it is apparent that the data developed on this basis provided the horrifying statistics that were continually reiterated during the campaign. According to the Commission, the center municipality would have 6 per cent of the territory, 2 per cent of the population, and 72 per cent of the tax revenues; the north municipality would have 37 per cent of the territory, 65 per cent of the population, and about 23 per cent of the revenues; the south municipality would have 5.7 per cent of the territory, 20 per cent of the population, and 4.4 per cent of the revenues; and the rural municipality would have 60 per cent of the territory, 12 per cent of the population, and 0.8 per cent of the revenues.[6] In the case of the 21 municipalities, financial data were advanced that only five would be able to sustain their own expenses.[7]

In the material available on the campaign, there is no indication that the supporters of the municipalist movement accepted either the four-city or the 21-city concept as a serious basis for organizing the state's local governments. They favored either a two- or a three-city system. A prominent member of the Social Democratic Party and former mayor of Rio, Marshal Ângelo Mendes de Mórais, actively pushed a proposal for two cities, one to be urban and the other to be rural and suburban. One of the three-city proposals followed somewhat the same pattern in suggesting the creation of an urban-zone municipality and two in the rural areas. Another used a geographic basis and would have simply divided the state into north, south, and center municipalities.

The most significant of the three-city propositions, however, came from the leader of the Labor Party in the state assembly, Saldanha Coelho. He suggested north, south, and rural municipalities. At first glance, the Coelho idea seems little different from the others; but the absence of a center municipality is really significant. What Coelho proposed, in essence, was to merge the center (with its 72 per cent of the revenues) with the north (and its 65 per cent of the population). Not only would the financial-supportability question thus be resolved, but two other goals would be served as well. It meant that the north would have a significant amount of money at its disposal. Also, the north would be a virtually certain political base for the Labor Party. The wealthier areas of Rio were in the south; and the claim of the north was that most state funds went in that direction from the conservative state government. Thus, a financially healthy north municipality would not only meet some long-held aspirations of that area, but

---

[6] "Carioca Decide se Divide a Casa," *O Cruzeiro,* April 5, 1963, p. 22.

[7] Raul Brunini, "Possibilidades de Manutenção dos Serviços Públicos Municipais," in Comissão Especial sôbre a Organização Municipal do Estado, *Subsídios* . . . , p. 18–19.

also would give the Labor Party a strong governmental unit from which to operate.

The drawing of the boundaries, then, was no esoteric exercise. It undoubtedly confused the issue for the lay voter; but this murkiness represented an important advantage to the opponents.

The Stakes

Winning a campaign in Brazil carries considerably more than policy significance. The holding of power is central to strong party organization; for decisions to participate in a political party are founded far more on personal interest than on ideology. The lubricant in the system is undoubtedly patronage. Beyond that, the government is an important source of funds for propaganda and other political expenses. Such expenditures are made indirectly, but it is clear that private giving is far less important as a means of financing campaigns than is the case in the United States. For these reasons, gaining office is central to survival.

No single party commanded a majority in the new state; and two parties, one laborite and the other conservative, struggled to attract enough support to secure dominance. The central prize in the system was control of the executive, in which resides the greatest share of power to distribute favors. In Guanabara's first gubernatorial election, in 1960, Carlos Lacerda of the conservative National Democratic Union won with 35 per cent of the vote. In the state assembly, laborites and conservatives were about evenly split; and decisions were made on the basis of shifting coalitions.

In 1962 the laborites showed greater strength. Their candidate for the lieutenant-governorship won by about 7 percentage points over the conservative. Also, laborite Leonel Brizola received the greatest number of votes ever recorded in the old Federal District or in the new state by a candidate for the Federal Congress. In the state assembly, however, the two parties were left with about the same strength.

Since Rio is a pivot point in the national system, political control of Guanabara has great importance. In some respects, however, its capture seemed more significant to the laborites than to the conservatives. The laborites had less a national party than the conservatives, and depended to a greater extent on strength in the big cities. Its members, too, undoubtedly demanded more patronage than did the wealthier adherents to the conservative cause.[8]

These considerations also suggest the basic political split between the north and the south of the state. While the north had by far the greater share of the population, the wealth and much of the natural beauty of the state (including most of its beaches) lay in the south. As a consequence, there was continual friction over the competing demands of the two areas; and, as is true in most large communities, it is quite likely that a higher level of service was being provided to the wealthier area.

The economic stakes in the contest tended to be rooted in two considerations: (a) a general reluctance to see any change in a system which was giving great emphasis to the economic development of the area; and (b) the fear of the effect of the multiplication of jurisdictions on the conduct of commercial and industrial businesses. With regard to the first point, the conservative Lacerda government had taken some strides toward the industrialization of the state. It had created a highly effective system of support for the financing of such ventures; also in other ways, it had been positive in its approaches. The Labor Party represented another ideology; and since most of the industry was located in the central and northern areas, there was the immediate fear of coming under its control. Even if there had been no such differences, the sheer increase in the number of units with which the business community would have to deal was not warmly regarded. Furthermore, there was the tendency to relate municipalization with higher taxes and thus with injury to economic interests.

The Arguments

An analysis of the two publications of the Special Commission on Municipal Organization and of articles appearing in the newspapers

---

[8] The Guanabara Labor Party, led by leader Saldanha Coelho, had bitter words with President João Goulart over the failure of the federal government to provide sufficient patronage in the state. See Carlos Amaral, *As Controvertidas Nomeações de Interinos para a Previdência Social em 1963,* dittoed, 31 pages. Mr. Amaral describes some of the factors that motivate patronage claims by the Labor Party.

TABLE 16. THE ARGUMENTS FOR CHANGE IN MUNICIPAL STATUS,
GUANABARA AND ST. LOUIS

In Guanabara	*In St. Louis*[a]
1. There is a need for more decentralization of government activity in the state.	1. Would increase possibilities for progress, economic opportunities, advantages to the entire metropolis.
2. Municipalities are a traditional part of Brazilian government and required by the Constitution.	2. Would improve chances for cooperation among governments, uniform services, righting of equalities.
3. There would be a fairer distribution of funds because each municipality would have control over its own collections.	3. Would allow for the improvement of services and solution of specific service problems.
4. Would promote greater efficiency.	4. Would increase the efficiency of government and would lower costs.
5. Would promote greater industrial development by making each community responsible for its own future.	5. Would increase industrial development.
6. A new approach is needed because the state government has failed to meet the problems of the area.	6. Would improve planning and zoning.
7. Rio's regional diversity should be recognized through the establishment of local levels of government.	

[a] The St. Louis summary is from Greer, pp. 69–74, 121.

between October 1962 and April 1963 shows that the opponents' arguments far outweighed the advocates'. Indeed, our analysis indicates that the opponents to municipalization advanced about 50 fairly separable propositions while the proponents generated only 13. Numbers in themselves are of course not greatly significant. In this case, however, they do convey a sense of the one-sidedness of the communications about the issue. In the publications of the Special Commission, for example, there was really only one essay, representing about 10 per cent of the total printed material, that was clearly favorable to municipalization. A good share of the remaining material was either directly or implicitly in opposition. The relative quantities were about the same with regard to newspaper space. Qualitatively, too, the opponents seemed to have the edge. Certainly their claims made greater use of research and statistical data.

Tables 16 and 17 provide a comparative insight into the kinds of arguments utilized in Guanabara, by contrasting the pro and con claims

TABLE 17. THE ARGUMENTS AGAINST CHANGE IN MUNICIPAL STATUS, GUANABARA AND ST. LOUIS

In Guanabara	*In St. Louis*[a]
1. Division of Rio's governments is not in keeping with its tradition as an integrated or organizational unit.	1. The costs of government would increase, taxes would go up.
2. Geographically, there is no basis for a division of Guanabara.	2. The plan would not decrease the number of units of government and would add a new one.
3. There would be many new expenses—more overhead for the new government units, more employees, costs of change, and so forth.	3. The new district level of government would be either too strong or too weak.
4. There would not be any new income.	4. Control over zoning would be transferred to the higher, district level of government away from the localities.
5. Taxes would have to be increased to raise funds lost by the state and to provide more support for the new municipalities.	5. Local areas would lose power.
6. Services would lack coordination.	6. Plan would favor city.
7. The police power, by Constitutional interpretation, would have to be assigned to the municipal level, which would lead to problems.	7. Plan would favor county.
8. Creation of the municipalities would tend to emphasize inequalities in the various sections of the state, promoting parochialism.	8. Proposal contains technical deficiencies.
9. Industrial development would be discouraged by the increase in the number of government units and by increases in costs.	

[a] The St. Louis arguments against are summarized from Greer, pp. 74–87, 125.

in Brazil with those made in the course of the campaign to create a St. Louis Metropolitan District in the United States. The St. Louis election was held in November 1959, and resulted in defeat for the proposal of a multifunction District.[9] In referring to the two tables, it must be remembered that the favorable arguments in Guanabara really involved

---

[9] Shortly after the St. Louis election, Scott Greer of the Center for Metropolitan Studies at Northwestern University made a rather exhaustive postelection analysis of voter attitudes and behavior. The result is to be found in his *Metropolitics: A Study of Political Culture* (New York: John Wiley & Sons, 1963).

a greater disintegration of the governmental structure, and those in St. Louis were advanced in favor of greater integration. The same differences hold true with regard to the negative arguments.

Theoretically, we would expect to find the greatest similarity between the St. Louis arguments "for" change and the Guanabara arguments "against." What we discover, however, is very little similarity between the two lists. In fact, the only claim that seems common to both these lists is better coordination. The Guanabara opponents declared that the coordination of services would deteriorate with municipalization; and the St. Louis people inferentially held the same belief in assuming that greater cooperation and coordination would occur with the creation of a Metropolitan District government.

There was one other important theme in common: localism. The St. Louis fear that local areas would lose power under the district system had its counterpart in the arguments for municipalization in Guanabara. Thus there seemed to be agreement that a centralized, unified system brings greater coordination; and the proliferation of units means greater local autonomy. It is not necessary that these propositions be true. If people believe that these are the consequences, they have their own reality.

In any event, the more striking finding is the similarity between lists that should be different. The arguments for change in Guanabara and St. Louis have familiar sounds, as do those against. Those seeking change made promises about the future. They looked to a better social and economic life. They believed in progress. Reform would bring more unity to the system. Services would be better and public funds used more effectively and more efficiently. The proponents seemed to avoid talk about taxes. Because they were proposing innovations in the governmental system, they tended to be vulnerable on this score. Thus we note reference to better services, more efficiency, and even lower costs; but no reduction in taxes.

The arguments against change are equally familiar. In both instances, new government units were proposed. Logically, these governments would cost money. Expenses thus would be higher and taxes would increase. It is interesting to note, too, that opponents did not typically talk about such things as progress, efficiency, and better services. They were defending what existed, and thus their main strategy was to express concern that things continue to be as good as they had been. Opponents of the St. Louis reform did do the impossible by claiming that the plan was both too strong and too weak and that it favored the central city government on the one hand and the county government on the other. In Brazil, the consequences were seen in functional, rather than jurisdictional terms. Claims were made that industrial development would come to a halt because of higher taxes and that traffic control would be hopelessly confused by municipal operation.

What was unsaid was also important. Though the principal actors in Guanabara recognized the political stakes in the plebiscite very well, there was really no public dialogue with regard to this aspect. To be sure, there were newspaper editorials which charged the Labor Party with the purely political motivation of seeking to reduce the powers of the governor. The Labor Party spokesmen let it be known that municipalization would at least begin to redress the balance between the north and the south of the state. Beyond such claims and counterclaims, however, nothing much was said. The same seems to have been true in St. Louis. Greer observes that the fear was great that the Democrats, already in control of the city, would enhance their political power. Yet this consideration does not appear as a frequently used pro or con argument in the tallies made by Greer.[10]

There is also a political dilemma involved in dealing with questions affecting the status quo. Politicians need to win. They cannot afford to be far removed from success. Thus there is a certain problem of prediction involved in taking stands on issues. The most desirable reforms will get little organized support when no one thinks they can win. Greer points out that the opposition in St. Louis was simply "the status quo mobilized" and that the "net effect . . . was to line up the political organizations—Republican and Democratic—against the plans. Regardless of merits, politicians like to back winners."[11] The same kind of problem arose in Guanabara, specifically in the Labor Party and in the smaller parties which tended to affiliate with it. As time moved on and defeat for municipalization seemed the more likely, the support of the Labor Party diminished rapidly.

THE DILEMMA OF THE LABOR PARTY

Success at the polls for municipalization of Guanabara turned very much on the Labor Party—the strength of its commitment, its ability to

[10] Ibid., p. 54.
[11] Ibid., p. 32.

get out the vote, and the volume of resources it could throw into the campaign. The Labor Party's official commitment to municipalization had been established when the regional directorate had voted it a "closed question," which meant that all party members were required to follow the established policy line.

By October 1962, however, conflict among party leaders had clearly come out into the open. Sergio Magalhães, who had just missed the governorship in 1960 and who was a federal Congressman, declared his opposition. Saldanha Coelho, the Labor leader in the assembly, reminded newspaper reporters that the question was "closed" and that Magalhães could speak only as an individual. However, the fact was that the power structure in the Rio Labor Party had been changed by the elections of October 1962. Several of the new state deputies were not committed to municipalization and insisted that the question be reopened for discussion. A leader of the attack was Ib Teixeira, who was one of the newly elected state deputies and who also was a columnist for the leftist daily newspaper, *Última Hora.* In November Teixeira ran several columns with titles such as "Important Questions to the Defenders of Municipalities" and "Municipalities and Demagogy." He stated that municipalization was not an "ideological" or "programmatic" question. Rather, it was a matter of "administrative order."

As of mid-November, it appeared that the leaders of the party were in real conflict on the matter. The vice-governor, the leader in the state assembly, and certain other influential Labor deputies still favored division; but Magalhães, Teixeira, and at least two other very influential deputies were opposed. In fact, the latter two asked, on November 13, that the question be reopened. Saldanha Coelho replied that reopening was possible, but that his position was unchanged.

By November 20, the newspaper *Correio da Manhã* reported that the Labor Party was in "violent crisis . . . creating serious problems for the leadership of Saldanha Coelho." Early in December it was claimed that only a "fraction" of the Labor Party leaders now defended municipalization. The majority was opposed. A former Minister of Labor, also writing in *Última Hora,* strongly attacked municipalization. In two different editorials, the *Correio da Manhã* questioned the Labor Party's motivations in seeking division. On January 27, 1963, *Correio* declared that the party's only concern was "to destroy the State through the division of municipalities." On February 3 the newspaper stated that "motive number one of the unfortunate project is political in nature. It is felt that by the installation of three autonomous municipalities the powers of the governor of the state would be diminished. . . . It is absurd."

Ib Teixeira also continued his attack. He was quoted in the metropolitan press on February 6 to the effect that "no political leader could advocate" division. It is "against the interests of the people and of social, economic, and administrative development." Also early in February Sergio Magalhães, the party's former gubernatorial candidate, was expelled from the Labor Party's regional delegation to the national convention because of his stand against municipal division.

Thus, about three months before the election, the Labor Party was having great difficulty in holding its own members together; and the likelihood was increasing daily that the municipal proposition would be soundly defeated. The showdown came at the regular weekly meeting on February 7, 1963. Ib Teixeira took the oratorical lead, declaring that he had seen a poll in which 70 per cent of the citizenry had manifested opposition to municipalization. He therefore claimed that his opposition was based on defense of the "prestige of the party" and his desire that Governor Lacerda not win a "false victory." The debate lasted two hours and the assembly leader, Saldanha Coelho, was defeated. Municipalization was now declared an "open question," meaning that members could exercise their own individual judgment. Worth noting, too, is the fact that the proposal to make the question "open" came from Vice-Governor Eloy Dutra.

The battle in the party, however, was not over. There was a good deal of "grass roots" support for the Saldanha Coelho position. A poll reported in *Última Hora* in early April showed, for example, that 11 of 13 members of the Labor Party's executive committee were in favor of municipalization; 81 of the 90 directors of the party were supportive; and the 14 Labor members of the state assembly were divided equally. Saldanha Coelho consistently sought to marshall this support in order to "close" the question again. He tried to enlist the backing of Leonel Brizzola, who had won a smashing victory in the race for the federal Congress in October 1962. Efforts were also made to have the election postponed, but these were all to no avail.

The Labor Party had a loser, a fact that was becoming increasingly recognized. No small consideration in this evolving situation was the attitude of organized labor. The First Regional Congress of Carioca Workers was held on March 18; and a committee recommendation to vote against municipalization was approved. It seemed that labor also wanted to maintain its strong, integrated statewide organization. The creation of municipal labor units would be a natural consequence of division. "[Between] the election of mayors and councilmen and the weakening of the union movement, we will choose a strong and united union," said the Confederation leaders.

Furthermore, the evidence was growing that Ib Teixeira's poll was, if anything, overly optimistic as to the probable vote for municipalization. The early April study by Professor Jorge Gustavo in Campo Grande showed that Labor Party members held almost as strong attitudes in opposition as did the conservatives.

By the end of the campaign, Saldanha Coelho was virtually alone. Vice-Governor Eloy Dutra finally announced his opposition two days before the plebiscite. Hércules Correira, a strong early supporter, denounced the proposal in March and suggested the creation of a system of "communes" in which the citizen bodies would be "deliberative and administrative." Thus did the Labor Party's once reasonably solid front wither away. The story has relevance here because it provides rather solid evidence of the manner in which goal displacement can occur in a campaign. The interests of the Labor Party clearly lay in municipalization and in the pruning of Governor Lacerda's powers. But survival came first.

INTERESTS AND STRATEGIES

The reversal of the Labor Party position was only the climax of a continuing growth in opposition to municipalization. The Commercial Association, the Federation of Industries, the labor unions, the National Order of Lawyers, the Brazilian Institute of Architects—all made statements in opposition. Newspapers of virtually every political complexion were directly or covertly hostile. Spokesmen for the Catholic Church raised questions. Even the Brazilian Communist Party, operating but officially illegal, endorsed the idea of "communes" and urged a "no" vote on the plebiscite. The Socialist Party announced itself against municipalization, as did the conservative Social Democratic Party, the largest in the nation.

Who stood in favor? The evening newspaper *Tribuna da Imprensa* announced on April 9 that it could find only two prominent political leaders who were outspokenly for municipalization. One was Saldanha Coelho; the other was the Social Democratic ex-mayor who had suggested the creation of two municipalities. No political party took a "closed question" position in favor of municipalization; and only two, the Labor Party and one of its splinter groups, left the question "open."

It is interesting to note that two of the interests which were very significant in the St. Louis campaign do not appear in this story about Guanabara. One is the suburban element. Even though districts like Campo Grande and Bangu could, with considerable legitimacy, be compared with the suburbs of United States metropolitan areas, there is really no suburban attitude or political posture in Guanabara. This lack is perhaps the more surprising in view of the fact that two-thirds of the respondents in the Campo Grande study had resided in the community for more than six years; and more than 50 per cent worked there.

The other absent interest element was ᵗhe ethnic group. Certainly, Rio has its racial mixtures; and despite what is frequently written, racial prejudice does exist. Such discrimination, however, is not expressed particularly through housing. The ghettos that do exist are more a function of economics than skin color. In St. Louis, on the other hand, Greer notes that the reluctance of the Negro to risk his power base in the central city was a factor of consequence in opposition to the District plan.

There are two governmental factors, as well as an emotional one, that may, in part, account for this situation. One factor is the existence of proportional representation, which insures that no vote will be wasted and thus provides an opportunity for interest-group representation in the legislature without the requirement that voters huddle together in a single electoral district. Also, Rio is one of the few cities known to this writer that really excites the love and affection of its residents. For them it is, indeed, the "marvelous city." It is a state of mind, and there is a need for identification with it. This emotional feeling, coupled with a more than 100-year experience under a single level of government, may account for the absence of a suburb-central-city conflict and also for much of the latent hostility to proposals for any type of dismemberment.

As apparently occurred in St. Louis, the advocates of change in Rio demonstrated little strategic effectiveness in waging their campaign. No effort was apparently made to build a broad basis of support for municipalization, either for symbolic or actual leadership purposes; and it was fairly apparent that hopes for success rested totally with the Labor Party. With the disintegration of that party's support, there was simply no campaign structure left.

On the other hand, the antagonists seemed to do nothing wrong. An unbelievably lopsided 20-1 victory undoubtedly colors any hindsight evaluation; nevertheless, the relaxed and yet insistent campaign of opposition had its independent merit. The antagonists began with a substantial hold on the state government itself. The conservative National Democratic Union held the executive mansion. This reality was demonstrated in the composition of the Special Commission on Municipal Organization, whose membership was split between the legislative and executive. With one possible exception, the governor's appointees were antimunicipal and so were the conservative legislators. As a consequence, the two documents issued by the Special Commission were controlled by the opposition and yet had the status of neutrality.

Governor Carlos Lacerda played a relatively minor public role in the campaign. Early, when it was not clear how the vote would go, there were reports that his public-relations counsellor had advised Lacerda to stay free of the campaign. It was feared that defeat would do harm to the personal prestige of a man who was already talking like a candidate for the Presidency of the Republic (he was nominated by the National Democratic Union at its convention in November 1964). By April, one newspaper reported that victory was so sure that the government had no need to wage a campaign.

The tenor of the opposition effort was largely negative. A sample of words used in opposition statements is particularly illustrative: "madness," "leading to chaos," "stagnation," "make-work," "impossible to administer," "total impracticability," "absurd," "ruinous," "chronic misery," "inadvisable," "retrogressive," "prejudicial," "sentence of death," and "multiplication of administrative difficulties." The labels were bolstered by a "technical" report that municipalization would not only discourage the development of new industries in Guanabara but drive away old ones. The state secretary of finance declared five days before the election that municipalization would drive up all prices and at the same time cause a depression in the salaries of state officials.

The ambiguity of the question to be decided also was exploited by the opposition. The four-cities concept, with its great inequalities in service obligations and revenues, was typically cited to show the impracticability of municipalization. Furthermore, there was the continual suggestion that all services would come under the municipalities. Indeed, the opposition propaganda seemed to have been able to shape the question as one of municipal government *against* state government, rather than municipal government *and* state government.

The success of the opposition in its strategy of negativism is made all the more perplexing when we compare it with the St. Louis experience. There the details of reform were carefully spelled out. The only problem was that no one bothered to learn about the plan. Greer reports:

. . . Around one half of the county sample knew of two major services which would be affected by the new district. Ten per cent knew its tax provisions. Thirteen per cent had a fairly accurate knowledge of its governance. Twenty-seven per cent knew that it would not abolish municipal government units. The rest was ignorance . . .[12]

In St. Louis, inherently contradictory campaign themes ("plan too weak—plan too strong") could be exploited to advantage by the antagonists to change. What these two experiences say to the would-be reformer about strategy is not clear. Apparently he is in trouble however he frames his proposal.

Unlike the opponents in St. Louis, the Guanabara opponents had a positive program. This was Lacerda's system of regional administration, launched in 1961. Whenever the argument for decentralization was brought forth, the opponents claimed as great a commitment to their idea as the municipalists claimed to theirs. However, they said that the need was for a system that provided local flexibility within a framework of top-policy coordination. Lacerda's government took actions that clearly kept the establishment and growth of the regional administrations in the public eye. For example, just before the election Lacerda moved his headquarters for several days to Campo Grande,

---

[12] Greer, p. 156.

where one of the first regional administrations had been established in June 1961. By election time the regional administration was therefore almost two years old; and Lacerda reminded the populace in public interviews that the community's resources accounted in only a small part for the accomplishments made. Earlier, in the previous November, a large festival had been held in populous Copacabana to celebrate the first anniversary of that regional administration. And in February 1963 Governor Lacerda announced the formal establishment of 20 regional administrations and three districts. At relatively regular intervals, administrators were appointed and the regions activated. The potentially strongest argument for municipalization was thus counteracted.

The Results

The ballot for the plebiscite of April 21, 1963, was very simple. It looked like this:

Ought the State of Guanabara to be divided into municipalities?

☐ YES

☐ NO

The results showed that residents appeared at the polls in very large numbers. Undoubtedly the mandatory voting law had much to do with the turnout; but even so, absenteeism has reached as high as 25 per cent in other states for important national and state elections. In April 1963, 82 per cent of the registered voters appeared at the polls, as contrasted with 85 per cent in state and national elections of October 1962. Of the total of 1,166,787 ballots received, about 20,000 were voided for various reasons and another 9,000 were blank. Of the remainder, the opposition amassed 874,137 votes to 49,707 for the municipalists. Nearly 90 per cent of those appearing at the polls recorded a "no"; and 94 per cent of those who registered an opinion (excluding the 9,000 who cast blank ballots) were in the negative. It was indeed an overwhelming pronouncement against change.

Analysis of the returns from the 25 electoral districts gave Labor Party leader Saldanha Coelho only small solace. The Fifteenth District, which had given Labor candidate Eloy Dutra most of his votes in the race for vice-governor, also registered the most "yes" ballots in the plebiscite. Even so, the figure was slightly less than 7 per cent of the total. The 5th District, which was located in the wealthier south and gave Dutra's opponent his largest vote in the 1962 campaign, registered slightly over 4 per cent in favor of municipalization. Thus the general direction of the vote was as might have been predicted; but the magnitude of the percentage of opposition votes was another matter. *O Globo* reported that only four members of the assembly voted for the establishment of municipalities. Thus ended Guanabara's brief flirtation with institutionalizing a municipal level of government.

CHAPTER NINE

BY WAY OF SUMMARY

Our modern-day technological society has placed increasing burdens on its governments. This is in part the consequence of more mouths to feed and more people to serve; it is also the result of a complexity and interdependence which require greater specialization in the system as a whole.

To meet these demands governments have gotten bigger. Bigness, however, brings dysfunctions. There is a tendency to worship the rule rather than the purpose. Individuals in the system frequently tend to lack motivation because they feel themselves powerless to affect outcomes. The interests of those served tend to be sacrificed to the interests of the servers.

While the ideology of a society may cause it to put much or little emphasis on various of these consequences, bigness is a problem in any social system. Its direct effects, however, are probably most keenly felt where the commitment to individual dignity and popular sovereignty is high. Democracies are required to consider ways in which the pluralism of the society is represented and maintained in its governing institutions.

A number of alternative approaches to this problem are possible. One approach of great significance involves the broad concept of decentralization, which means exactly what the word appears to suggest. Instead of lodging all power at a single point in a system, that is, centralizing it, decision centers are scattered throughout. Decentralization involves delegation of decisions. Simply to remove "doing" people from a given physical location does not signify decentralization. They can still feel as if they were in the same room with their superiors. The same is true with governments. Units may be geographically dispersed without seriously threatening strongly centralized operation. In the

United States the classic example of this phenomenon was, for many years, the U.S. Post Office.

In a number of democratic societies, strong institutions of local government have been regarded as the essential element in the decentralization process. Yet the simple creation of local governments does not mean that decentralization has been accomplished. The power to decide is still the key. Further, we must recognize that decision power must be construed broadly. It naturally must embrace a substantial area of freedom in which to act; and it also implies the capacity to command the resources and capabilities necessary to make the choices desired a reality.

The navigation of a course between the two extremes of governmental anarchy and absolute dominance from the center is certainly not easy. This difficulty is perhaps best seen in the approach to metropolitan-area problems. In the United States many of our metropolitan communities have created liabilities for future generations by their refusal to accept any kind of restraint for the good of the whole. On the other hand, there are great urban areas in other parts of the world in which centralization is complete, and the needs of individuals and neighborhoods have been submerged.

As if the problem of finding an appropriate course between the extremes were not complicated enough in itself, difficulties are frequently compounded by emotions that cloud such issues. There is also a tendency to oversimplify. Americans, for example, are prone to assume that strong local governments are the only way to achieve plurality in the total decision processes of the political society. In Brazil, however, the utilization of varying parastate organizations to provide a variety of services represents another form of decentralization, which is sometimes labeled "deconcentration" because it does not involve delegation of power from one level to another.

In this same context there is sometimes a failure to recognize the existence of stages of national development. In one Middle Eastern nation, Americans helped draft a local government law that provided for considerable autonomy; but the law could not bring about vital, viable local institutions. The whole structure of leadership recruitment and maintenance was lacking. Furthermore, the nation still faced threats of dismemberment from powerful tribal groups. Understandably, the voices at the center had important arguments for the rather rapid curtailment of the powers of the local governments.

On the other hand, it is necessary to recognize that myopia has been strong in decision makers at the center. Charged with the "big look," these people find it almost impossible to accept any conflict or contradiction in the system. They do not see such conflict as the price that must be paid when people or groups are free to behave according to their own interests or understandings. The maturity with which the Yugoslavs have approached this problem is particularly noteworthy. Since World War II, the overriding goal in the Yugoslav Communist state has been the improvement of material well-being. Until 1951 this improvement was sought through a highly centralized system. It did not work for two reasons: (a) it did not contain sufficient rewards to induce strong individual motivation to work; and (b) it could not develop a monolithic decision-making apparatus able to make the big and little choices with equal rationality. To avoid these problems, in the early 1950's the government undertook a considerable decentralization to the municipalities and to the socially owned enterprises. Today, local government units have the freedom to be different from their neighbors. It has been a daring experiment, but it has worked. Yugoslavia has achieved tremendous increases in standards of life since 1954; and the most striking aspect of this feat seems to have been the great emphasis placed on local autonomy. Furthermore, the events of the very recent years have chronicled significant political changes as well.

In addressing the problem of decentralization, Brazil has a number of imperatives that are important primarily for their political aspect. In the short run, the growing service expectations of the society must be handled. The big cities pose special problems, particularly those cities whose population is expanding much faster than their economic base. Indeed, it is ironic that raw power tends to concentrate in exactly the places where the problems of providing service are most difficult. The boiling point is low, and the potential repercussions great.

Yet it is not just a matter of keeping the urban masses placated. The long-run question is most serious. If we accept the commonly held view that local governments are training grounds for political development, it is important that there be motivation to participate in such systems and capability to do so. However, such evidence as we have suggests that Brazilians are alienated from their local governments.

They do not see them as producers of outputs that they prize, but as distributors of rewards to a selected few. If Brazilians continue to have such attitudes toward the government with which they have the most immediate contact, can Brazil expect its citizenry to participate in a move toward greater political development?

The answer to the question seems clear. Decentralization is needed to achieve both political and economic goals; and of these, the political factor is by far the most important. Despite its intermittent vicissitudes, Brazil is inherently a democratic society. However, democracy by definition is not government by the elite or for the elite. It assumes broad concern, participation, and responsibility in the affairs of the polity. It is exactly at this point that the evolution of democracy in Brazil has had its greatest blockage. There has been relatively little involvement in either subject or participant roles. Irresponsibility in the subject role makes it difficult for the government to perform its output functions; lack of activity in the participant role makes power abuse easier and leaves the government an instrument for the elite. While these are problems which occur at all levels of government in Brazil, they seem to be the worst at the municipal level, where closeness and understanding should ease them the most.

From the economic point of view, Brazil has major problems of infrastructure. It seems unlikely that a centralized command system can either produce the capital or the efficiencies necessary to meet the growth needs of the urban society. The local community is going to have to set many of its own priorities, make its selection of penalties to be incurred, and participate in the struggle to improve the quality of life. The experience of Yugoslavia suggests that there are optimizing motivations that can be tapped with much profit.

If decentralization is a necessary part of the governmental scene in Brazil, the basic concerns of this book have meaning; for our purpose has been analytical. A focal interest was to examine the ways in which the municipalities have been relevant to their environment and thus have promoted the decentralization of the political system.

The fact is, though, that much is not known about the decentralization process. Endless arguments compare the merits and demerits of local autonomy; but scholars have speculated relatively little, and have done even less research, on the dynamics that promote decentralization and make it viable. This book starts from a fairly simple premise: The grass roots become important when elements in the environment in which they are located think they are important. That is, municipalities achieve institutional status when they are valued for what they do. With such prizing, their boundaries become more meaningful and less vulnerable to attack; critical segments in the environment are more interested in providing inputs to them; there is more attention given to the ways in which inputs are selected and converted into outputs; and the provision of outputs to the environment is made easier. Most importantly, with this value comes autonomy, defined as freedom to interpret environmental demands and to respond to them. An institutionalized government, then, would perform important services in its community, elicit the support and interest of its constituency, secure adequate resources for its activities, make decisions in such a way as to reflect the pluralism of the environment, and find its maintenance eased by citizen support and commitment.

In the attempt to make these concepts operative, I have relied heavily on systems theory, which has led to three basic questions: (a) What does the municipality do for its environment with what kind of effect? (b) What does the environment do for the municipality? and (c) In what way does the municipality take the energies it gets and convert them into valued outputs?

Given the open-system nature of the municipalities, the relationship with the environment is crucial, as I have consistently pointed out. If there are forces in the environment pushing for centralization, values that prize local autonomy will obviously be in conflict. Under these circumstances, institutionalization of the grass roots is not likely. On the other hand, as either latent or manifest supporting elements are found in the environment, questions about outputs, inputs, and conversion mechanisms assume significance in the search for means by which the institutionalization of the organizations that represent these values can occur.

It should be pointed out, however, that those values in the environment which would be expected to prize the things municipalities do may not in fact be supportive of their institutionalization. A value commitment to improving urban-metropolitan services does not necessarily mean that the municipalities are regarded as the systems from which such outputs will come. Indeed, the rural character of the bulk of the municipalities makes such an identification difficult to establish. There is no one level of government in Brazil that is perceived as uniquely dedicated to the problems of the urban dweller. Functional boundaries that would serve to specify the nature of the municipal contribution to urban values are therefore difficult to establish. As a result, the values in the environment that would seem most likely to support the institutionalization of the municipalities do not necessarily do so.

Within this context, it has been useful to think of the municipal problem as involving two systems. One is the municipal government itself, called the community municipal system. Its principal transactions are with its community. The other is the national municipal system, which is the collectivity of municipal governments. The municipalities are in effect a subsystem of the total political system of Brazil.

The two suggested systems are important only for their conceptual convenience. What happens in each of the community municipal systems will be regarded in the total political system. Nevertheless, it is important to take a look at the individual municipality and to consider the character of its relationships with its community, the types of outputs it provides, the demands it makes, the demands it receives, and the supports that are obtained. As we come to comprehend the processes by which the municipality becomes prized in its milieu, we will have taken the first steps toward an understanding of the dynamics of decentralization.

Attention to a national municipal system is useful because it reminds us that many environmental decisions of great importance to the individual municipality are taken in aggregate terms. To put it another way, the manner in which the larger political system relates to the municipalities will have a great effect on their institutionalization and hence on the level of decentralization in the society. An analysis of the inputs to this national municipal system, both in terms of the constraints placed on the municipalities in seeking local supports and in terms of the provision of resources from higher levels, has seemed particularly revealing. Since 1934, when the national municipal system first began to achieve recognition, the official commitment to the institutionalization of the grass roots has very considerably exceeded the supports provided.

This book closes as it began. The problem of getting full participation in today's large and intricate organizations—both public and private—is profoundly complex. And it becomes the more complex as we include responsible democracy among the values to be sought. While we are coming to the realization that command systems are neither politically desirable nor economically efficient, we have hardly begun to face the meaning of a pluralistic approach to patterns of organization. That confrontation must take place in our universities and businesses, as well as in our governments.

INDEX